T0072402

THE HUMAN MIND AND BELIEF 3 - RELOADED

THE HUMAN MIND AND BELIEF 3 - RELOADED

Why Is the Human Mind the Way It Is?

EUGENE G. BREEN

authorHOUSE®

AuthorHouse™ UK Ltd.
1663 Liberty Drive
Bloomington, IN 47403 USA
www.authorhouse.co.uk
Phone: 0800.197.4150

© 2014 Eugene G. Breen. All rights reserved.

No part of this book may be reproduced, stored in a retrieval system, or transmitted by any means without the written permission of the author.

Published by AuthorHouse 08/18/2014

ISBN: 978-1-4969-8877-5 (sc)
ISBN: 978-1-4969-8897-3 (e)

Any people depicted in stock imagery provided by Thinkstock are models, and such images are being used for illustrative purposes only. Certain stock imagery © Thinkstock.

This book is printed on acid-free paper.

Because of the dynamic nature of the Internet, any web addresses or links contained in this book may have changed since publication and may no longer be valid. The views expressed in this work are solely those of the author and do not necessarily reflect the views of the publisher, and the publisher hereby disclaims any responsibility for them.

Other Books By Eugene G Breen
The Human Mind and Belief – Opening Shots
The Human Mind and Belief – Unplugged
The Screech Owls of Breast Cancer

These lines are dedicated to those I know with illnesses of all sorts.

Contact author at www.mindandbelief.com

CONTENTS

OVERVIEW

The world and all that's in it. The future and the past. Time, and being, and beyond the wildest frontiers of the human mind. The material and the abstract and the spiritual. The good and the bad. The entire universe. Is it all just for us? "Scientists have reported" the newsflash goes in 2035 or 3520 "that they have discovered the roulette particle. It is as we know the source of everything and the product of the final theory. It was the centrepiece of the science of creation discovered 35 years ago by WH Whodunnit and long thought to be within our grasp. Patents have already been issued to two labs in Honolulu to commence creation. Sceptics say this is not creation de novo but a smart voodoo gimmick aimed at unnerving the Russian China science consortium into thinking the Americans are ahead. As of yet nothing has been created. Observers say it is too early yet. Mr Whodunit when interviewed (who has capital in the Honolulu lab) said he was confident we would have definite news soon. Ends"

No matter what we hear you can bet your bottom dollar that no one will ever create. Create means to make something out of nothing. Everything we ever see or witness comes from something. There has to be a substratum, a raw material for anything to be made out of it. That seems obvious. We haven't even discovered nothing yet! Nothing is absolutely nothing and everything in existence is something. Science has not yet discovered nothing or nothingness or how to "make" nothing. It is a rule of life, that something gives rise to something else. Nothing gives rise to nothing unless you can create. Man has never created. Man will never create. "Nothing" means: no rays no particles no attractions no gas no light …..and no existence or being. Take a chunk of this "nothing" and breathe being into it. Make flies and wheels and men. The easy bit is making men and wasps, and the hard bit is making being. You can only make being or life de novo out of nothing if you can create life and being. It is not irrational but for us it is definitely way out of our range.

Believers in God say that God created everything. Therefore God can do it. The other question is why does God do it? The answer is out of love for man. Love is the driver and cause of creation. It has to have a cause and why else would God bother to do all that hard work? God is pure love with a capital L. That is the pinnacle of God's essence. Man also can love to a lesser degree and isn't it true that love even in this life is creative? Does love not create a powerful atmosphere, energise people to achieve the unachievable, build the house and life of their dreams, and so on? Doesn't love build bridges, bring healing and understanding and drive people to work and get going, and engender families and presence in their community? But is that creation? Well there was nothing there before and now there is a family and a sense of peace and mutual support. But you had people and communication and opportunity to build on something. Correct. Even still, that "lovin feelin" is new and it was created out of … yes people and human contact and the activity of the human mind and will and spirit. "Let's create something special for Tommy's birthday" and so they think and plan and imagine and get inspired and "create" something very special that will blow Tommy away. This is human "creation" but it does start from an idea and human endeavour. Real creation does things like that without the starting materials. Creation out of nothing is not irrational. It has happened but we don't understand it and we cannot do it.

How outrageous do we need to get? Is anything possible? Skunks playing Sudoku? Elephants flying? Men multitasking? Women reversing cars into tight car spaces? Once a thing is rational it is in theory possible and doable. What can never happen is an irrational thing. Who knows what is rational? Things happen that defy rationality, or at least our understanding of rationality. People recover miraculously from illness. People live admirably in marriage for over 50 years. People sacrifice their lives for a person or a cause. Creation. Creation is not irrational. It's amazing and we can't do it in this sense but it is not against reason. It is beyond reason. The sun is so bright you cannot look at it and yet no one would deny that it is bright. It lights up our universe. The truth is so clear you cannot comprehend it. Love is so strong it empowers you beyond natural powers. Will we ever understand everything? NO! Yes? Will we find the cause for life and earth and everything at some stage and have the key to life in our hands and rewind time and bring back the dead and all live for ever happily? NO! Yes?

Why not? Because there is more to it than our level of rationality and our little minds. We need to be honest. We need to see who we are. A big issue is how we got here, who made the place, why do we have minds like we do, why are we unhappy here, and all the other things that happen to human beings (Love, struggle, pain, injustice, joy….). This is not science. This is knowledge and we all learn a lot of what we know from others. We'd better listen in and learn what all of humanity is telling us about ourselves and the world. Past and dead and gone humanity are saying "we suffered, we died, we cannot communicate directly with you, but look at what happened to us!" Living humanity are saying mostly "we are suffering". There are 50 million displaced persons on earth at a minimum at this point in time. This does not count the millions in starvation and poverty. This does not count the millions with illness. The tortured and neglected. Is there anyone OK? The minority on earth are middle class suburban.

More than white or dark matter or quarks or whatever, this sweltering mass of suffering humanity is a big issue. Why? Does it matter if scientists discover the cause of it all if we are all sick, or hungry or dying? Does it matter to the dead? NO! There are a lot of writers out there throwing dust in God's face. The God delusion, the non-existence of God, the evolutionists, the deniers of God. There are internets full of false logic and argument confusing people and telling them there is no God. These people never ever answer the direct questions about all the important things about man and life and death. They go on forever (?) sowing doubt and detracting from creation and God and the meaning of life.

Enough of that! These people have to be answered and some of what is in the following pages has them in mind. The rest of what is here is written to try and throw some light on the big issues concerning man and the lives of everyone.

So what have we got? We have the human mind............ and any collateral? The only source of collateral is religion. Science and history also help because what religions say is real and pertains to earth and is verifiable a lot of the time by science and history and geography etc. For example Catholicism actually says God became man and lived on earth 33 years and his actions were chronicled and witnessed. Sounds like you need go no further if that is true. This is exactly the problem. Even in his own day his countrymen witnessed his acts and heard his words and crucified Him. Nowadays what is happening is that it is denied that he lived, or that He was God, or his miracles are denied and said not to be factual and historic. Denial is the only answer of people who do not accept that it happened. I accept it and here goes!

The number of unanswered questions without God is enormous. The number with God is well…..very small and very manageable. With God as the cause and creator, everything makes sense. It fits our way of thinking and is personally satisfying. Our thirst is quenched and our heart is restless no more. I wonder why? Maybe we are made for God. Maybe that's what we are missing! People who love God are happy, they suffer, they die but they are convinced they have the truth, and they are at peace. Now study that! A person who says he has the truth, will die for it, and is happy and wishes for nothing more, and is a decent respected worker, is a big challenge. This is not just one special person. There are and have been millions. These are serious people. They are asserting serious things. They live according to what they believe and die in that belief. This must mean something. They were not stupid. They were not deluded. They were not hysterical. They were and are genuine believers and are very decent and loving and happy people. Why not ask them about the universe and the cause of everything!

Life in general is divided into three groups. Those who believe in God and that He created everything and keeps it in existence. Those who don't believe in God and who say everything just is the way it is and that it evolved over time. The third group is those who don't care. Let's take group one the believers in God. They say God created everything. God can therefore create. If God can create it must be doable. How does He do it and is that the answer to all questions? Mathematicians and physicists say that everything emerged from a dot sized "particle" that banged due to energy and other forces and thus we have the universe from the big bang. The process is ongoing and the universe is expanding still. This dot is something and where did it come from? What was before the dot? The answer is God and God is the author and origin and creator of all sciences and dots and intelligence and He obviously knows how to create and maybe some day He will tell us a little of how it is done.

Without positing a creation you knock your brains out figuring out how everything appeared, how we are in the middle of it and why, and where it is all going and why. This is all being done blind folded and without the trump card, which is that of creation. This quest to explain everything on purely human terms and with human rationality is doomed to failure, because for one reason science and technical and mathematical advancement is all to do with discovering what already exists, and describing it in maths or physics or chemistry and copying what is discovered or revealed by nature, and it is a retrospective activity mimicking what nature decides to let it see. This is not to belittle scientific or technical advancement but to say what is happening. We should discover more and more and be in wonder at the amazing design of everything but also realising that the ultimate scientific explanation of the material universe and all the answered mathematical systems converging on the final equation may not be revealed by "nature". Our way of working is that the more money you throw at something and the more people engaged in researching something the quicker and more likely you are to get answers. This system works most of the time. This is based on the so far so good will of the revealing hand of "nature". If nature closed shop and said "enough of that, I'll blind them for a while, or for ever, and show them no more of my wisdom" then the game would be up for scientific advancement. Discovery is like a veil being slowly withdrawn from the inner workings of nature and man's rationality getting to work on the new revelations and so advancing knowledge. Without revelation or discovery we would stand still. The ultimate exposure of all there is to nature and the "process" of creation at its inception may never be revealed. It is like advancing to a point and being in touching distance but being forced to advance half the distance to go, and then half of that distance and then half of that until you never reach the point. Our exploration and advance in knowledge is not at our pace. We do not decide when we will discover anything. We take what we are allowed and what is shown to us.

Besides all that we haven't even mentioned man and his explanation. What a crazy being is man without a loving creator! How do you ever think of understanding man with all his joys and sorrows and justice and right and wrong and limited life span in evolutionary terms? All the information about the material universe pales in significance to the stature of man and his cause and destiny. Science and maths and all human disciplines cannot capture the life of a man or woman. Without explaining man and woman everything else is useless and wrong. The totality of all life material and spiritual past and present and future must have a coherent unifying and simple explanation. Evolution has none of these qualities. Relativism never even tries. Creation is your "man".

ADDICTION

Addiction has become a pejorative term. It means that a person is in thrall to drugs or drink or whatever, and that they can't control it and that their lives are usually pure misery. A bad place to be! They waste time and money and relationships and their only goal in life is to get their next fix. They talk, eat, and sleep the addiction. Their repertoire of thought and behaviour is constricted to the world of their preferred substance. They are chronically ill. They have possibly an irreversible cloying and dependence on a substance or activity like drinking or gambling or internet or even TV.

Chances are, we could all get addicted to almost anything. The usual is that the substance or activity is attractive for starters and it pulls us in. Otherwise we wouldn't get addicted. The genetics of addiction cause some to be more at risk than others. Addiction can run in families. Addiction doesn't need a genetic predisposition and anyone can become addicted given enough exposure to the substance or activity. It is like an obsessive thought that you know is stupid that comes from yourself and that you just can't stop. The idea and reality of addiction is a pointer to how we can, and do become attached to things. Addiction could be called the worst form of attachment.

We also become addicted to our own thoughts and egos and ways of doing things. We are just hard wired to ourselves. This also has the damaging aspect of addiction because it is not good for us. We are supposed to be sociable and contribute to society and family and work. When we are self-absorbed these go out the window and we live in a world of our own. We isolate and distance ourselves and become loners in our heads if not in fact. This addictive tendency we have highlights our stickiness. We get attached. Life being full of possibilities makes it crucial for us to be aware of this weakness and strength. Strength when we become attached to something worthwhile and for our good and that of others. Bad when we become enslaved to something that damages us and others.

A child addicted to sweets or internet (hence the need for counsellors and psychologists). An adult addicted to food (hence obesity epidemic we are living through). A financier addicted to cocaine or power. A jockey addicted to weight loss. The scary thing about all this is that we could concertina our lives into a struggle with a substance and even maybe die from it. Are love and hobbies and interests addictions? No, but they are of the same family or spectrum it could be said. The spectrum of attachment. When children attach or bond with their mothers or mother figure they develop well and eventually become independent and stable. If they don't bond because of problems with the mother they become unsure of themselves and develop dysfunctional attachments to people. This leads to issues in adult life. They have relationship problems confidence and esteem issues and possibly depression and anxiety.

We need to be vigilant so that we do not get attached to the wrong things. Even better if we purposely search out and fine tune the really good things we want to be attached to. Attachments tend to be enduring because of our nature. They don't have to be but often and more often they are. We have worked at them and begun to like them and feel loyal perhaps to them and our screen saver is to be attached rather than not. In other words unless something happens, like we consciously decide to break an attachment, the chances are that it will endure and possibly even grow stronger. Love is probably the best and most enduring good attachment provided it is to a legitimate person.

Animals also get attached and addicted. I'm not talking about lab animals getting addicted to cocaine or whiskey which they do if exposed in research, or of babies being addicted to their mothers preferred substance when born, but of social cohesion and flocking and herds and being together. Animals generally stick around together. House pets definitely get attached to foods and walks and chairs and biscuits. They even watch television with their owners. Proof of this was when one man came in and said he was tired watching the Olympics late at night and his dog was also tired because he was up watching it as well!

We are what we eat. The human body turns over every so often. The different cells have different life spans. All in, we go through hundreds of new bodies in the course of our lives and we are not at all the same person we were this time last year! All that goes in to replace dead cells is food and water. We are organic. I suppose we knew this all along but when you think about it, it doesn't seem to gel with what we imagine ourselves to be. We somehow think we are the same person and in a certain sense we are not. Not, that is in the material sense. We have completely changed and we are now just burgers and spuds and meat and French dressing acting up as a human being. Imagine that. How is that possible? What changes a tub of muesli into a talking walking human being? Now that is amazing! There must be some converter plant inside of us that changes food into human. Some magic process that completely transforms basic mater into human matter. How can a burger think or laugh? How can a cauliflower sleep? Yet that is all we are - cauliflowers and burgers....or are we more?

OK you put petrol into a car and it moves and people get carried around the place. The difference with animals and humans is that the petrol just doesn't give the energy to move the thing it actually becomes the thing. Burgers become men and women. This is being a bit disingenuous but it serves to highlight the amazing quality of the human person. It shows that the spectacular abstract and spiritual life of the mind and the consistency of the self identity is based on a very material and ordinary material i.e. what we eat. It is interesting that you can get old and wizened, or fat and breathless, or drunk and disorderly and it is still you! You change dramatically throughout life but it is still you. The integrity of the person is preserved. This must be a spiritual or abstract thing, because everything else about the person has changed many times in the course of life. The welter of intellect and art and science and thought is all based on a substance made up of peaches and pears and fast food. How can this be?

You can chop bits off the body like legs and arms and breasts and colons and you still are the same guy! The brain is like the liver or kidney in that it is nourished by blood and food and oxygen and is a material organ. It is supposed to be the seat or source of abstract life. Abstract life is not nourished by chips or fries but by ideas and by urges and by mental activity and life. The process of becoming addicted can be both physical when the body craves something and also spiritual when the mind craves something like a loved one or an idea or an ambition. We are like flies attracted to fly paper and then we get stuck on it. This tells us something about ourselves. We are not isolated immune singletons that do not interact. We are very prone to being attached to almost anything and to a certain extent our life is a battle to attach well and avoid harmful attachments. Addiction is the hard core of this tendency.

The reality of addiction or attachment underlines our real vulnerability or strength to adhere to something or someone or even to an idea. We are sticky. We form bonds and these can be lifelong and enduring. They can decide our lives and lead us to put everything else in second place. We have a sweet spot and are affected especially by other people. The way they react to us, the way they deal with us, the way they love us, affect us deeply and even permanently. We fall in love. We get hooked. We decide. This human characteristic is part of our nature and every healthy person has it. Why? Why all this attachment? Why are we not like cool calculating robots? Maybe it has to do with man's ultimate destiny. Maybe it has to do with why we were made. Maybe it means we are destined to be attached to the object of our desire for ever? It is definitely a strong urge. It is present in everyone. It is only partially satisfied in this life. Is there a full or permanent exhilarating version? There should be because that is what we desire and long for. This desire or longing isn't fake. It is real and true......and as such must prefigure the definitive expression of this faculty for ever. Something to think about!

THE DEAD

Where are they now? All the dead. There must be billions and trillions of them. They were larger than life when they strutted their lives in broad daylight. They were invincible some of them. They were rock stars and emperors and princes. They were speech makers and social shakers and people of substance. They were also number 657 or 348 in mental institutions or prisons. They were starving and destitute and abandoned and hopeless. Are they no more? Was it all a mirage?

What about all the effort and suffering and achievement and success? Gone? What about all the sacrifice and self-denial and altruism? Disappeared? The love and the emotion and the warmth and friendship…just a mist that has burned off? What about all the human endeavour and invention and advancement? A guffaw? Where is all the desire and struggle and war and peace? Where are the people who lived in the house at the corner?

They all went into the ground or the sea and decayed into clay! They are no more. They are never even thought of nor remembered nor spoken to. They are as if they never were as far as we are concerned and as far as we can see. They are now non-being for us. The reality is that we are doing the same thing. We are playing our role as we see fit and as we can. We are tossed and thrown by life events and chance and are at the mercy of the next virus or car crash or tornado. We will fare no better. We will be no more soon.

But are they really gone? Was it all a natural season with no more than a day in the sun? Is it all meaningless and evanescent and did they all get it wrong? They sweated their guts out trying to make a go of life, some for good and some for themselves and some for selfish interest, and was it all a sham? Should they all have sat back like the animals and taken it easy? Should they have stayed in bed?

What we do know for certain is that their bodies and physical presence are gone. That is only half the story. What about their minds? Does the mind have a life of its own once up and running? Does it still need a personality and a body? That is not definite and on the contrary it is very logical and plausible to posit that the mind is an independent entity, like a space craft that gets out of earth's gravity, and just keeps going on its own.

Taken from another standpoint we can say that we don't count really, because we created nothing. We did not cause life and we did and do not sustain and control life. We live the life we "inherited". We are powerless. We are creatures with a beginning and an end (in this life anyway). Who is watching this whole escapade we call life? Who made and sustains life? Whose idea was it anyway? To say that "that's the way it is", or to say "it is nature" or to say "it is evolution" is like telling your four year old that babies are dropped into the house by storks! It is not an answer.

The mind is immaterial and as such it cannot disintegrate and die according to our understanding. To die and decay a thing needs to be composed of matter or components that cause the thing to disintegrate and decay when they are separated. The mind is simple and is not composed of different components, and as such and as science and philosophy understand it, it therefore has no principle of decay. It cannot be reduced to simpler substance. It is as simple as it gets. Ideas are for ever. What has happened is eternal. It cannot disappear. This is according to our reasoning. All we can do is hypothesize and use our reason as we have been given it. Our reason works on earth. It sets rules it governs our thought and behaviour (most of the time), it is dependable and consistent and functional for life on earth. We are caught in a time warp and the reason and functionality of our brains and body are suited to life on earth. What happens when we leave earth? What happens when our bodies die? That is exactly what happens…our bodies die and go but our history and our will and our imagination and our desire and our abstract and spiritual lives go nowhere. They are all still very much alive. They are bodiless now but they cannot disappear and die because they are spiritual realities that do not require matter to be (to exist).

This is all great stuff but how do you know? Ok how about chance, sudden death, disasters, murders and freaks of nature, what are they? How about bad luck, good luck, and unpredictability? What are they? How about the entire panorama of the human mind, what is that all about? How about we know nothing about what is going on? How about we are like animals in a zoo and the game keeper knows all about what is going on? Does someone know where the dead are, why we are the way we are and what is it all about? Does this "person" know where the dead are and what they are doing and why? That would make sense to our reasoning. To say we don't know, and that it is all an automatic evolutionary cycle of nature, with no reason or purpose, contradicts all our reason intimates and suggests to us. It is nonsense and irrational.

Oftentimes we cannot precisely prove a fact but we can logically deduce the fact. For example, gravity. We see things fall to earth and deduce that there is a power or attraction there, and we are right. What we cannot do with this example is actually see the power and the existence of gravity or of big G or little g …but they do exist. When you see a rainbow and don't see the sun for example you deduce that there must be a powerful light shining at a particular angle through water vapour to give the rainbow effect. You deduce there is a powerful light but you cannot see it or prove it exists…but it does. When you see a child neatly dressed you deduce an adult dressed it but you can't prove it…and you are right, an adult did dress it (unless the child is way beyond the normal!). The same applies to the universe and life and man. The place is full of hints, and rainbows and signs that something is behind it all. Signs that it all makes sense. That there is design, and our rationality is actually correct about this as well. The only way to get at the truth about life and the universe and man is by getting all the collateral evidence and signs and by using reason to deduce the power behind it all.

For starters, what makes no sense is to say that it is all over at death and that once dead, life stops for man. Life is such an unfinished business with so many unanswered questions and loose ends and scores to be settled that death is like stopping a film half way through. Nothing makes sense. Nothing makes sense on an individual level or on a mankind level. For example justice for all is not met at death and some have all the luck and others have been terribly treated. Reward and punishment for lives lived needs to be squared and be seen to be done. Recompense for lives of suffering or illness or poverty needs to be given. An explanation for what it is all about and who did what needs to be promulgated to satisfy rationality. These all point to a life after death. Life down here is irrational to our human minds. There must be a real proof and levelling of issues at some time, and since it does not happen in this life it must happen elsewhere.

Getting back to the dead, they must be all terribly disappointed with the whole life business and must be crying into their drinks and beating their breasts at the tremendous let down of the entire experience. They have to be beside themselves with anger and rage at being given a wrong steer and spending all that time and effort pursuing a false dream. They must be inconsolable. Those that lived good self-sacrificing lives now find that the selfish and embezzlers and rapists and murderers etc. are just as well off as they are. The entire cauldron of dead humanity must be pulling its hair out and wishing they had a second go at life. This time they would make no mistake. It would be party time all day all year all the time.

A second scenario for the dead could be that they don't exist anywhere and are absolutely annihilated and like as if they never existed. They don't feel, don't think, don't talk….they don't exist. They are like cardboard boxes you discard and that disappear with no trace. They don't have a mind or brain. They don't have a body. They don't have a memory or conscience, they don't eat or sleep. They are no longer on the radar and no one remembers them. They are the same as the dead cattle and antelopes and beetles. The reality of life for plants and humans and bugs is the same. They all live whatever duration they are built for and then form compost matter. A big question mark about all of that!

Reincarnation is a theory or belief of some religions where the dead are said to get another life as someone else. This makes reasonable sense from the meaning of life point of view. That it all just doesn't stop at death and that there is more to it and that our actions do matter and can impact on future lives we may get. This explains some aspects of the reason behind human life and the reality of justice and conscience.

To this point then we really haven't rationally explained the dead and what they are up to and why they are dead! What is this thing about death anyway? Why death? Why not live forever? Why not be always happy? Why have a conscience? Why truth and right and wrong? Why crime and punishment? Similarly you could ask why don't football games go on forever? In football there is a beginning and end (death), there are rules, there is justice, there is conscience, there is truth, there are fouls and red cards. It is a mini life! There is even a referee, someone who makes and enforces the rules. There is a rule making body - FIFA. Come to think of it golf is the same and motorsport and all games. Maybe life is just a game but just a little longer and with life and death penalties. That fits. But who wins the cup? Who gets to ride on the open top bus through town? Who gets relegated? Who is the referee and who sets the rules? This really is a mirror of life. Why do things stop? Why is there always change? Why is there temporality? The dead can help us tease out these whys.

If the dead are truly dead and no more, nothing makes sense. The entire football game was and is a farce. We are truly on a mission to nowhere and life is just a parcel fallen off some passing reality that doesn't maybe even notice that the universe fell off the back of its being! We could be a chunk of junk offloaded by some passing life form or excited being who was heading to some championship football game of a much bigger reality. We don't make sense and are like a whinging orphan in some forgotten nursery. Could this be the case? Could it be that some amazing being is now actually searching for us to bring us back to mother ship and explain everything to us? Maybe there is a grieving enormous baby being that is pining for his universe that he lost and which he got for? Christmas? And that Santa Claus his ginormous "father" made for him to play with. If the dead are dead well then this guy better hurry before the rest of us are no more and he forgets how to make us again!

This is outlandish but not irrational. It is an attempt to rationally explain life. This is the type of stuff you do come up with if you say the dead are dead. If you say the dead are dead and that that's it, well then you have abandoned rational thought. Yes we could have dropped off the back of some other being's tricycle and that in itself means we are part of a bigger reality than what we see down here. It means there is someone more than us out there and someone who owns us. Maybe this being is the referee and law maker and ultimate cause and meaning of everything there is. To say the dead are dead and no more takes all the meaning from life and means that nothing is worthwhile and we are caught in a dilemma. This is nonsense.

The majority of people think the dead are alive! The majority of people live as if they will never die. The majority of people use the reality of their own animal death as a deterrent and guide on how to live. We cannot explain how immaterial things like ideas and thoughts and willpower and memory die because they are spiritual or abstract realities and in this life to die you need to be composed of physical matter. The principle of death and decay only pertains to physical matter. The soul or mind cannot disintegrate because there is no simpler substance for it to descend to. As such the dead are dead in body but not in soul or mind. This underpins the rationality of one of the reasons why death? Why death because life is not the finished product but a trial run. If this were not the case life would be eternal. Life in the body as we know it is temporal. The only explanation why this is so can be gleaned from the components of life and seeing how they all fit with a temporal structure.

Conscience, right and wrong, truth, effort, self-denial, love and hate, success and failure all need to be explained. These and other aspects of life all occur in the context of a temporal reality. There is a beginning and end date to live these characteristics. What suits our mind and rationality is to understand the rules of the game and seeing that it all makes sense. To say the dead are in fact alive spiritually has everything going for it. It means there can be a transparent accountability of what really went on during life. It means there can be a settling of all kinds of scores that it was impossible to square in life. It means that justice and truth can be done and be seen to be done. It means that love and fear and hate can be explained and appropriate rewards and penalties attributed depending on performance in life. It means that all religions and beliefs can be exposed for their truth. It means that change and temporality and effort can all be understood and come to their purpose. It means that the human heart can be explained and fulfilled and put to rest. It means that relationships can be restored and mended and perfected. It means that happiness is real and that life for ever is real. It means there is a design and purpose for life. It means that our deepest dreams and desires and loves can find expression. It means temporality and change and death can be overcome and left behind as shadows. It means you do and can live forever. It means you better find out how to score highly in this life because that is the standard you will live at for ever.

THE LIVING

Human life, and all life is tantalising! Bird life, dog life, fish life, get a life! To *be* that is what it is all about. Every breath you take every move you make every thought you think are all signs of life. They are sustained and nourished by the energy and vibrancy/zing we call life, much like a landscape is sustained by a hidden spring of water which allows vegetation to grow and flourish. Humans, animals, plants and everything that "is" feeds off this life elixir we can call "being". It is like an invisible presence that we don't see or hear or touch but that we witness in its effects all around us. Switch it off and everything would disappear and not only fade from view but be erased from reality. Nothing would "be" anymore. New life, old life, all life is plugged into this wellspring of being. It is an enveloping presence throughout the entire universe and penetrates everything that exists or "is". Death in this sense is not the opposite of life since decay and recycling occurs…into organic matter or debris of some sort which also is a form of life. After all we are nourished and grow and live thanks to organic matter as food. The plants grow and live thanks to debris and compost, so there is some sort of life in dead matter. The real opposite of life is non-existence or annihilation.

The origin of being is a mystery. The origin of life in all its forms is also mysterious. Being and life are almost the same thing. It is like producing a rabbit out of a hat. What a strange thing to produce a rabbit without life! That would be a stuffed rabbit, and creation or the producer of being and life doesn't do stuffed stuff. Being brings something into existence and life starts the motor or gets the thing to act as it is designed to act or to be. It is the power for movement and responsiveness and lights up all the inbuilt faculties of the "thing". Being doesn't do fake things.

We have never seen fake reality and it contradicts our reason. The origin of being and life just keeps churning out all kinds of things. We have never doubted being or life and we trust the supplier. He has a great track record and has never let us down. We are really stargazed and dazzled by reality and everything we see and experience, and we never ever stop and say "Hey all this life stuff, all this activity, hey wait a minute, we are being conned. This is not real, it's all a game. We are caught in a false world. Everything is fake. It is we who think everything is real and that we are in charge. Think about it we are being fooled". We never think that way. We don't, for one reason, because we are too busy checking out this new house or car or computer i.e. this world and all it contains, and our excitement at our good luck and our curiosity completely distract us. If we did doubt the world and its veracity we would really be basket cases. We would have absolutely no ground under our feet we would slowly go crazy if we were lucky.

We are vulnerable, very vulnerable and we got invited into this big shot's place for a short stay and he could turf us out if we got arrogant or too smart. He has the power and he knows that, and so he realises our fragility and dependency on his good will and support, and he has not fooled us or tricked us because, what's the point?..... And also because that is not why we are here. We are here because the source of being and life for some reason wants us here. For some reason we were fashioned the way we are. For some reason it is a real life and death game. It is a puzzle and we have to find the clues. We are constantly in competition with ourselves with others and with the world. We definitely are unsettled and are driven to act and improve and advance. We are not the final product and we have not reached "peace". Happiness is the pot of gold at the end of our rainbow and restless will we be until we get there. This is why we describe life as a puzzle or game because it is like a quest for a holy grail. When defined in its essence it is the effort and struggle to achieve endless secure happiness and peace and fulfilment. That's what we think but maybe we don't have the full story. We are players and not the manager or the owner, and maybe the prize is absolutely beyond our wildest dreams. Maybe the pauper is to be made a king in fact and the ugly duckling a beautiful swan.

Being and life are always true and genuine, and this confirms our trust in the basis of life and being, and in the fairness of the contest. We enter into dialogue with being and life by living. We probe and ponder and gaze and think. We are gifted with an enquiring mind, and since everything is true and genuine we have no reason not to use it, and be happy we are not on a wild goose chase. Life and being guarantee the authenticity of everything we see and experience, and of existence, and of the way things are made including ourselves and our minds. We also are not fakes, we are not stuffed rabbits and so as far as our reason allows us, we absorb all the truth and genuineness around us and so we get some real clues about life and being.

It is like as if we have been airlifted onto planet earth or the universe and we discover all this activity going on. We are amazed looking at everything. We landed in the middle of a show that is full on and we have a complimentary ticket and a welcome. We are like children fumbling through Christmas parcels. We really haven't a clue how we got here or how the entire universe and planets and everything got here either. We are excited and throw ourselves into discovery mode and do science and geography and reading and writing, and like an orphan adopted by a wealthy family we take everything as belonging to us now.

We have been at this quite a while. Some say man is around 7 million years and that he grew up in Africa. Others don't give as long. (Neanderthal, Clovis, American man etc). Whether or which we are adopted. We were not at the design stage of this enterprise. We did not draw a circle on the deep or marshal the stars in their rows. We did not invent speech or sea or land. We did not develop the human mind in a lab. We are agency staff. We were recruited when everything was already up and running and we will be let go when we have done our bit. We are hired hands with a start date and an end date.

Life is short and you should make the most of it, so says a well-known piece of advice from a parent to a son or daughter. Life is what you make of it, is also common wisdom. You don't appreciate your health 'til you lose it and you don't appreciate money and what you have got unless you earn it the hard way.

Life is a funny old thing! We awoke into it and we didn't ask why and we didn't have hand act or part in it. It happened. Our parents know something about it but even they were surprised to see us. Wow it's a boy. Wow it's a girl. Wow what is it!? Humans beget little humans and bees beget tiny bees and washing machines beget clean boxer shorts. Monkeys do not give birth to kangaroos nor do dogs give birth to elephants. I wonder why? Is it like that throughout nature? Well yes! Each species begets its own type.

This is all a work in progress and we didn't kick start it. We are just in the middle of it and are actually part of it. We did not invent or create or generate ourselves. We had nothing to do with it. We don't know how we got here. We don't know who or what we are. We are an enigma. We inhabit a twirling sphere teeming with "life". If the lights went out and the heat was turned down we would all perish and become organic dead matter. We would be frozen stiff. Best to keep the sun shining and the globe turning as it seems to create the right climate for us to survive. A fraction of a degree either way for the earth's tilt and we are history. What a world! Who thought of it? Was it always like this? Will it always be like this?

We see new species and new bugs, but they all evolve from extant animals or bugs. We haven't seen a new being de novo without a precursor. We have not seen creation. Everything we see has its basis in what already exists. The creation event has stopped it seems. Yet the living process continues and old things die and new things replace them. Everything gets its day in the sun (literally!) and then is no more. (i.e. the sense of being that intact unique being with all its characteristics). Here today gone tomorrow. Strange!

"And the lights all went out in Massachusetts" is the famous song by the Bee Gees which goes on "the day I left her standing on her own". This may be a hint as to how the lights could go out on the universe. If we leave her standing all alone…if we lose love. How about that! What are you on about? Well the light in and on our lives is a freebee. Love is for another chapter, but isn't it a power house of energy and warmth and drive and affection and …life? As far as we go as human beings isn't the experience of being loved or of loving someone really, a different world altogether? Isn't it a real turbo boost of life? Isn't it a quantum leap in the quality of being and life? Interesting! We will discuss this further in a later chapter. A life without love would be lights out to some degree. Total blackout would be absolutely no love. Getting back to our topic, we are just there (alive on earth) and we absolutely had and have nothing whatsoever to do with it. We were created. We are extraordinarily complex beings and there are billions of us, and what do you know, no one knows what we are, where we came from and where we are destined for. No one knows where the planet and universe came from. No one knows anything.

We are like bullocks in a field. We didn't make the field, we didn't set up the fence, we didn't fertilise it….but the farmer knows a fair bit of all this. Ask him. Who then is our farmer? Who fenced us in and fed us and watches over us? Who will bring us to the mart and when? Are we being fattened for some other crowd who will gorge on our entrails over chopped eyeballs and salted spleens!!? Why not? If we didn't have a brain or mind we might be ok. We wouldn't have to think about such things. But we do have a brain and mind and these ask an awful lot of questions.

How do you define life? Well, it is experienced in movement and generation and responsiveness. It can be of animal, plant, material, or human form. It has a beginning and an end as far as individuals are concerned. Planetary life that is animal, vegetable and mineral, depend on the conditions of earth and its atmosphere. It could not survive outside this milieu. It is extraordinarily varied and of enormous simplicity and complexity. It is really well organised. Animal and plant life needs food and air and water and warmth to survive. They grow and change and get old and die. Human life is of a higher order than any other life form we see and includes a spiritual and abstract component. It is the highest form of life on earth. Humans are the top of the pile and control much of what goes on, on earth, much like a site manager controls the building site for the boss. Human life is goal directed autonomous to a degree and really advanced life. It is self-reflective and rational and free and dependent (on others and food and warmth etc). Humans are aware of themselves and of others and of everything that exists and is visible to their senses or reason.

Life is like electricity it turns things on. It must come from somewhere and must be "generated". The big thing is that it only lasts for a while and then it disappears, at least for the individual. Generic or life in general continues with new trees and animals and humans. Individual trees and animals and humans die and disappear. Life is temporary and it changes all the time for individuals and it constantly gets "older". If there was no time it would not age or change…. possibly. This business has been at it now for a long time. Some say man dates from 7 million years ago. Some say there was a big bang 14 billion years ago and that it all has occurred since that and that the universe is constantly expanding and expanding and who knows what comes next? What happened before 14 billion years ago? What happened before the big bang? What caused the big bang? There must have been something because you cannot get a universe, big bang or no big bang …out of nothing. Some mathematicians and physicists think everything actually did come out of nothing but they can't say why.

How about the 23 ice ages? The last was 13,000 years ago? When is the next and what caused them? Where did the mind blowing organisation to exquisite detail and consistency in nature all come from? Where did our DNA with its millions of base pairs all working in synchrony come from? Where did all our neurones and nerve connections in our brains, trillions of them….come from? These all breathe life, and work according to their nature, and we didn't do it. Planet earth left to itself just gets old and disorganised, and yet life forms have an order and organisation absolutely contrary to this disorganisation. Animals must be from another laboratory you may think. They are not earthly, as in they don't show increasing disorganisation and entropy and chaos. They seem to hold true to their design and functionality and mating and eating and living patterns. These patterns are orderly and instinctual and seem to be enduring over time. This seems to contradict the planetary progression toward decay and chaos. They are like foreigners on a dying planet. They have the hallmark of a masterpiece and a superior ability and intelligence when compared to organic nature. Humans are even better! They advance and increase in numbers and knowledge and order. They are the ones that put most order on the planet (the stupid ones are also the ones that damage the planet most due to pollution and waste and disorder). The reality however is that animals and humans do decay and die like the planet and so the process of entropy holds true even for them.

It seems then that animals and man are true to the original design, as good as new creatures when born and young, inhabiting a decaying habitat. The evolutionary process understood in its correct sense even suggests that man and animals are even getting more complex and sophisticated with the passing millennia. Planet earth has a best by date and like long life batteries it just takes longer to die. All living things die. Animals plants humans. Earth is dying as well and becoming fatigued and worn out. Much of it is already dust and debris and what was gleaming new iron and zinc deposits is now recycled old motor cars and fridges. The material resources of the world are finite. There is only so much oil, so much tin and so much radon. It could be said that the world renews itself and you get new water with desalination, new food with GM production, new oxygen with its manufacture. All these processes are tapping into scarce and limited resources and eventually all the good stuff will be gone. There is no new creation going on. There is no limitless source of material or energy. Yet the world of life seems to be going in the opposite direction. There does seem to be an endless supply of new plants and animals and humans, but maybe the supply is also finite and has an end date. The supply of humans and animals and plants is possibly reaching a peak and who knows maybe we are on a downhill supply curve like the earth and the entire universe. How so? Could it be like a zoo where all the animals reproduce and eat all there is there and then the place is bereft of food, and to survive they have to eat each other. That is of course if there is no game keeper who forks in new food all the time. We don't seem to have such a game keeper to keep the earth and planets topped up. We are like midges around an earth mound. We, like midges are short lived, whereas the mound and earth live much longer. Why we and the midges are replaced and the mound gets longer to live is curious. The earth is like our house and we come and go but the house stays, but it too gets old and dilapidated and falls down. The earth is getting dilapidated too.

What has man created or invented to compare with the human brain or the chicken or the amoeba? If there was a competition for ingenuity and discovery and genius and man pitched up against the maker of man or horse or earth, no prizes to guess who would win. It is the master craftsman against a splinter of his creation. Life must have had a beginning. There is no reason to think that life arose spontaneously. We have never seen this happen. We don't understand it and it is illogical. We cannot even conceive of the idea of nothingness. What does "something" mean? We haven't got the mental fire power to comprehend this type of thought. We are temporary on earth and we have the apparatus to live on earth for a short while and we don't need the extra gigabytes of hard disc to plumb the depths of reality and life. We don't have to "do life", we just live it and our brains are purpose built for that. Nature as we see is functional and those things that are not needed die away like the appendix. Our minds don't have to create, they just have to live the life received. Someone else creates. The creator needs a much more powerful brain because He has a harder job!

OK, we can't create. We have never done it and never will because it is beyond our capacity. Where then did life come from with all its beauty and complexity and organisation? Are our brains kitted out to probe this issue? Is such a question beyond us? Well yes and no. Yes, we can reason about it and try and make it understandable to our way of thinking. No, we cannot make life. We do and can pass it on in generation but we have never seen and we cannot fathom how anything would appear without a cause and without raw material being already in existence to go into its making i.e. create out of nothing. Even dark matter and black holes and matter we cannot see or sense or measure, it all exists and we did not create it. This is based on our tried and tested rationality. Creation is beyond our limited power of reasoning to understand, but it is an idea in our heads and it is not repugnant to reason - just beyond it. It could occur that some day we will understand the possibility of creation out of nothing a little more clearly. It is possible that some day we will have more data pointing toward creation. It is possible that we will understand better the idea of nothingness and achieve more steps toward the final simple formula or theory of everything. And what then? If this is incorrect then our reason is faulty and everything is stupid............... We can only work with the minds we have and this is usually within the frontiers of our reason. Our reason cannot explain why life is as it is and where it came from and how; or maybe it can....if unbiased and true. We should at least try with the lights of our limited reason to study and learn about the universe and ourselves and see how far we get.

We do however have more powerful search engines in our minds and persons which function beyond straight laced cognition and basic rationality. These faculties we call instinct, experience, innate knowledge, human wisdom, intuition, inspiration and the overarching pathway of life that we tread, we don't know how, which guides us unknowingly toward our denouement. The three pillars of belief and hope and love are surreal "instruments" in our quest for reason and meaning, and drive our search for meaning to absolutely superior heights. Harnessed to all our other faculties (mentioned above and below), they are like nuclear fission in our minds and souls and make us capable of vaulting over the conundrums of basic reason that our cognitive faculty baulks at. It makes us see beyond human expressed reason and enables us to grasp and assimilate realities light years beyond our basic rationality…..Simple examples of this are the effect of pain or suffering on a person; the effect of being loved; the experience of endurance; the tautness of the virtue of hope in our souls/minds; the pangs of remorse; the effort of belief…these all speak to the inner core of a person and go way beyond basic rationality. This gleaming architecture in our minds (formed of belief, hope, love, instinct, experience, desire…) can and does launch us way beyond our "human capabilities" to ponder the origins of life and love and being and what it all means. This is real life and even though only intellectuals may be able to articulate it, the simplest of souls live it often to even sublime degrees. These powers enable us to capture the possibility and idea of creation, even though we haven't the "how to do manual" to hand yet.

Pure reason is insufficient to explain life. Other faculties have to lend a hand. As mentioned these are our will, our emotional life, our memory, our desires and passions, and our deep longings, and the experience of living our lives. These are rich sources of a deep knowledge and unspoken wisdom that often shapes our behaviour and our drives and lives. We experience deep seated tendencies to strive for goodness and we experience deep draws on our nature toward evil. This has introduced two new concepts - good and evil. Again, we didn't invent them we experience them. They shape us and have powerful effects on us and we will discuss them in another chapter.

Putting a search engine into the human mind over the millennia and crawling through it what you find is the same tune played with different hues and tones. The lyrics of popular songs, the words of poems, the themes of great literature all reflect the human spirit. They yell out the human yearning for completion or consummation and fulfilment of the human condition. They all speak the human heart's toil and hope and turmoil in the temporary human frame. The flames of love and loss and humour burn perennially in these lines, and the light of hope forever shows the way to man. Spin it all down in a centrifuge and you find the sediment of all human life to date settled in the shape of a question mark! Like the tribe of pygmies in the jungle who were too small to see where they were going, and who used to have to jump up often out of the long grass to get their bearings shouting "where the f are we" giving rise to their name, The Wheredefukawi Tribe, man too has to jump up often and ask who the f are we?! Sorry about that, anyway, yes a question mark.

What is left at the bottom of the centrifuge is a distillate of all we ever felt and thought and hoped and loved, and unless a shaft of transcendent light illuminates it all and casts the image of the true face of man for us to see, we are left piteously poor with a makeshift dull sediment of what we are without help. The good news is that the light does shine and the question mark is erased and in its stead a cascade of brilliance and tangible joy envelops the shining face of the new forever man (and woman!). The real seed of man is not to be found in his gene pool. It is not in his prowess or achievement. It is hidden from our eyes in his spirit or soul or mind. His real identity marker is in his spiritual nature. He is a spirit parading down the centuries in his working clothes, his body. His body is intrinsically part of his being and existence and he could not exist without it, but it is only half the story. His soul is the animating principle of his being. His soul lives on and it is this that catches the light of transcendence and illuminates his passage through time and shows the answer to the question mark.

Man yearns for, strives for, and is destined for eternity and joy. It is written all over him and is evident in his life and his history, and is captured in his poetry and literature and song. Man is meaningless without this third dimension. Without the explanation and fulfilment of his every dream man is not rational or understandable. His mind and body have soldiered long and hard down the years. The body dies because that is what happens to organic material but his mind doesn't die. Like Siamese twins one is cut off and dies and the other survives but is distraught and frozen without the other, and likewise man's soul is paralysed without the body. The real grand finale with the orchestra rising in volume and pitch is when the soul rides back into town and picks up the old bones it once knew and loved (old flame) and they both embrace and in the embrace become new again "Forever 21." This is what the transcendent light shining through the sediment of man's history shows and this is the destiny of the living. Not everyone gets this acclaim and rides into the sunset happily ever after because there is another image cast by the transcendent light through the sediment of man. This image is horrible and dark and repugnant. This image stinks and burns and yowls and cries interminably. Yes it is also alive, yes it is also a union of soul or mind and body, but no, it is not a happy occasion. It is hell. "Hear ye! Hear ye! Read all about it. The interminable fight between good and evil, the gallant hero against the dragons and demons. See how he smashed them to hell. Hear ye! Hear Ye! Read all about it "The demise of man. The tragedy of fallen man burning in hell forever. Don't ye go there folks! Terrible!" This we will revisit in another chapter.

To cut a long story short, life and living mean something and are understandable or else they are mysteries, and worse than that they are stupid. They do exist we live them we suffer them and we think about them. If human reason and the wisdom of the human spirit (experience, inspiration, hope, belief, love, yearning, intelligence…) are all we have to understand life and living, and all of these faculties consistently over the centuries point toward good and evil, toward, reward and punishment, toward fulfilment and eternal bliss…well what are we waiting for? Nothing else is going to happen. What has happened will happen again and we will die just like our ancestors. This is our last best chance. Our head and heart together are our only equipment to get us home safely.

PERSONALITY AND THE PERSON

What kind of definition of person do you want? Do you want a legal definition or a philosophical one or some other type of definition? The real definition is the important one because true law follows or should follow what is true and real. The idea of person and personality are important because when one is deemed to be a person one accrues all the rights of a human person. This has implications for people who are not compos mentis or in a coma or even in the womb. To tease out when and where personhood resides it may be helpful first of all to state the obvious and say where it does not reside. By personhood we mean being a human person and by personality we mean all the effect that being a person has on oneself and on others and on society. It includes the impact, presence and influence that a person has on basically everything including themselves. Personality is the clothing and way of being and interacting of the person. A horse has personality but not personhood. He may be affectionate, loyal, frisky or stubborn. A cat is often sly and selfish, choosing the sunniest spot and caressing to get more Kitty Kat. A dog seems to have more personality. He/she can be affectionate, good company, playful, vicious and stupid!

I have yet to meet, if "meet" is the correct verb, a foot or a hand or an elbow that impacted on me in the same way as a complete person! The point being that personhood and personality, which differ from each other, do not reside in body parts as such. You do not experience the presence of another "me" when you contemplate a body part. Another way of considering things is to ask how much of the body do you have to remove until the person becomes diminished or even disappears? People may disagree on this and say that organs and body parts are not important and what really matters is the presence and personality and history of the person. A comatose person in intensive care is very much a person objectively speaking no matter what anyone thinks. It is a fact and a real person exists even though incommunicative and in a coma. They do not display personality in this state (usually), but wake them up and there they are again, warts and all in their now tattered and worn out body and personality. Such a comatose person is still very much Paddy or Teresa for those who knew them during life, but possibly not for those who meet them for the first time as a comatose patient. He/she could acquire personality for them if the life and family and friends of Paddy or Teresa were introduced and acquainted with the caring staff. They would be part of Paddy's or Teresa's world and would flesh out the type of persons both were in life. "He was a lovely man" or "she was a delightful person", and in this way it introduces a life that may assume "virtual" reality for the caring staff who never knew them when they were well and alive. We all experience this sort of thing when we read a biography or see a documentary about someone. The account may affect us deeply and even lead us to emulate them or change in some other way. This occurs in the absence of a body, person or materially lived experience with that person. This suggests that personhood or personality is even outside the physical body and lives on in the "ether" when the person is well dead or absent. Cremation ashes or a grave may have the same effect by recalling the life of the deceased. Memories can be very real and affect a person in such a way that the dead person comes alive in some way for them.

It seems then that personhood is not always or even ever circumscribed by the body. Another view is to say that without at some stage having a body you could never have a personality or be a person. Once a person has been a person (if that is not a tautology) their person and personality live ....for ever! They have made a shape in the indelible wax of life which is eternal and can never be erased. They have lived and breathed the air of life and have done things and thought and all that is now converted into their pdf which cannot be edited. It is frozen in history and also in the minds of those who knew them and who hear or read about them. To generate personhood and personality a human being has *to be*. Once a person has *been, has lived, the reality of their being has pushed a story and a living shaft through the abstract and immaterial world and everlasting world of ideas. It cannot be undone.* **A**s Katie Melua sings about the 9 million bicycles in Beijing "There are nine million bicycles in Beijing. That's a fact. It's a thing we can't deny like the fact that I will love you till I die." Let us get back to the basics again.

You could not "be" without a body. You don't need a full body. A head and thorax will do the job, as we often see with amputees. A parent suffering with dementia for example, also may retain personality and personhood even though cognitively and mentally deficient and lacking a substantial part of brain substance. This suggests that a functioning brain is not required for personhood and personality to be present. A person must have lived at least for some time to acquire personality or..........must they? The absolutely zero starting point for any glimmer of personhood has to be the very first appearance of a living human being. Personality seems to be a secondary phenomenon understood as coming after the initiation of personhood. Is a zygote a person? Is a foetus a person? Is a one minute old baby a person? Is a demented old lady a person? Is a disabled child a person? What is the hallmark of being a person? A person is a ring fenced self contained human being. A person is not calculated in years in size in intelligence in continence in looks. A person has the genetic profile of a human being. A person has dignity and is respected for what he/she is – a human being. A person is not a particular number of cells or a particular dependency type (dependent on food or drink or dependent on nursing care or a ventilator or even dependent on a placenta or a womb). A person could be and in fact always is at some stage just one cell! Welcome to Mr or Miss Zygote! Why not? No reason why not.

Some people are full of character and life and "personality" and are big persons. Others pass through life without hardly impacting on anyone or anything. Some leave legacies and memories and change life for others in a relatively enduring way. Others were never known and are forgotten - perhaps the vast majority of people are like this. The impact factor of a person is the effect of that person's life on others and on life in general. It presupposes personhood. Personality resides in a human person.

In fully blown adult life it is in the human mind that the person and personality reside principally. Therefore what we are describing are impressions or experiences or effects that others have on us, and how we define and categorise that experience. You could have personality and personhood if you were always alone. What impact or reality or influence has a human person who never has any contact with other humans is a difficult question. There are examples of such people being reared by wolves and they are supposedly wild and ignorant and uncommunicative verbally and require rehabilitation. The evidence for the existence of such feral children and adults is scant and none is scientifically proven and researched, but they are persons with personality though the latter may be severely regressed and blunted.

Personhood and personality requires "someone" who has lived. How long? Some time? This also could apply to the unborn. An unborn person is very much alive in the parent's minds and hopes and dreams and as such constitutes a life in their eyes and hearts, even though not yet born. The understanding of personhood in the broadest sense is the vision we hold of whether a person exists at all or not. The word "someone" implies some person. There is absolutely no reason why a zygote could not be a person. No infusion of personhood takes place at any subsequent stage in development. The idea that personhood implies that the human has the capacity to take on responsibility is a different idea and concept altogether and is not a necessary condition for personhood.

Personality pertains to the level of impact or vivacity of this person. We could also look at the objective reality of the existence of personhood and personality in its own right regardless of onlookers. There is a person with personality present regardless of what we or anyone else thinks. Is there a "quid hominis/mulieris" or human spark in the most primitive and isolated human being? The answer has to be yes since every member of the human race is a person with their own personality. Most people fit the description of homo/mulier sapiens but quite a few don't! Rationality is a moveable feast. Some have it a while and then lose it through illness like dementia and others with brain damage never have it. Rationality is useful because if you have it you definitely are human but if you don't you still could be human. In fact a fair proportion of the human race are irrational….children below the age of reason, demented people and those suffering with incapacity from whatever cause, drunk people and those strung out on whatever!

It is like the joke about the physician and surgeon out shooting duck. The red setter raises the game and the physician says "It looks like duck, it flies like duck, it quacks like duck. I think it is a duck" The surgeon says….Bang! (shoots it). "Check it out and see if it is duck"! Suffice it to say at this point that the germ line holds true i.e. once a human always a human. The signature of being human material is the origin of the being. Once a being is begotten of human stock it is a human person. DNA profiling helps but there are millions of people with unique genetic profiles be it trisomy21 or mutations or deletions or extra X or Y chromosomes etc. DNA is therefore not invincible in this area, and may in future not be the gold standard for defining humanity. Like rationality it is helpful when you have 46 human chromosomes but their absence doesn't mean the being is not human. It is the origin of the being that determines its nature. When the components of the zygote are from a human male and female sex cell it is a human zygote.

These days with in vitro fertilization, mitochondrial transfer and with the terrible spectre of human-animal hybrids the definition of what it means to be human is soaring way beyond basic DNA sequencing. The bottom line about DNA and its variations is that if any of the DNA of a being is of human origin it demands respect since it at least partially emanated from human stock. How much DNA do you need to be human? Who knows? In time it is possible that other markers for human material will emerge but DNA is the best at present. You cannot be a human being without also being a person. The traits and characteristics of a well crafted person are the fine tuning and honing of the personality which is the clothing of the person but not its essence. The essence of the person is the dignity and reality of their being human of whatever development or stage of life. The difference between a body part and an embryo is that the embryo is pluripotent, or a total human being in potency, whereas a body part is just a part. It is possible to consider that the embryo is a person already in the lives and minds of those that know him. Whether becoming a person is a stage in embryo development is debated. It doesn't seem to make sense to say it is a person at week 10 or week whatever and thereafter, because nothing any more significant happens at week 10 or any other week, that makes it attract personhood. The coming together of the ovum and sperm and the coalescing of their DNA to constitute a brand new DNA profile at conception seems like a profound moment and all that is needed after that is to let nature take its course. This is the first moment of a new life and if this new zygote is a tiny human it is reasonable to say it is now also a tiny person. Several court cases have recently shown that the foetus has rights and it successfully sued for damages done to it in utero. A search on the internet for foetal rights shows that many countries have assigned rights to the unborn child. After conception all the embryo needs is protection and nourishment. The essence of personhood comes from the intrinsic reality of being a human being. Being acknowledged to be a person is nice but it is not essential for it to be true.

What would an isolated person think about? How would their mind develop? Do we have examples and evidence of what actually happens or has happened to such people? They have an innate way of being which is genetically proper to them but further development of their personality would be difficult without company. The point being pursued is that a human has an innate personhood regardless of anything else, such as the presence of others or not. Our impression of another is our and other people's own inner experience of that person. It is the total impression or experience another causes in us and as such emanates from the person and impacts on us. By looking at the impact, feeling, thought etc that another person causes in us we can study the nature of the stimulus, in this case another person. Could we say that every person has a unique effect on us or do we react to others like a herd of cattle i.e. the same for all, a generic yellow pack response "oh yea that's another human" type of response. We experience individual reactions to individual persons and more distant to TV shots of amorphous crowds of people.

One may ask does a crowd have personality and we can identify a crowd of football supporters and we identify and react too them depending on our interest in football; we see a stampede of frightened people fleeing from danger and we may identify with them and pity their plight "it could be me…it is me!"; we see a crowd of holiday makers and we may envy their luck and so on. Crowds therefore may strike us as having personality and even personhood depending on what we know about them, but the overarching impact is the recognition of other "me's". We find it difficult to ignore another person and so it should be. By ignoring and being immune to another one ignores ones very self. This is unnatural but possible, does occur, and is not unusual. Ignoring others means not acknowledging their innate dignity as persons and failing to recognise another "me", a wayfarer in human garb plodding life's weary way. It also would question our own fidelity to our own true nature, that of also being persons. It is a denial of self and of our own personhood. People with Asperger's Syndrome, with autism can do this due to illness. People who hate can do this through hatred. People with self absorption or serious preoccupying problems on their minds can do this out of distraction. It is not usual for people to not acknowledge other people but it is unnatural.

There is a wide spectrum of human behaviours or characteristics that we could annotate like a biologist and make a spread sheet of all possible human characteristics and tick off each person into these categories. This is possible. Doctors annotate profiles for cardiac status or health status or personality type and the whole behaviour of a person is capture-able and quantifiable and assessable. What is not quantifiable or visible is the mind or soul or personhood of a person which is the real core of the human being. This unseen quality is contained in the body of a human and it vivifies the body and bestows personhood and personality on it. A human body is animated by a human person. The presence of a person or a human soul or human mind is really the sine qua non for the existence of a human person. One could therefore say that to be a person you should have the dignity and spiritual shape of a human being and as much of a human body as is required for this human spirit to dwell in……as least as far as this life goes (the body is not a second class citizen and is "half of the person").

Could this be a simple zygote? Could this be an emaciated comatose body? Could this be a severely mentally and physically disabled child? Yes, yes and yes! The hallmark of being human, of being a person is the mind and spirit of a human person, and its body no matter how defective it happens to be. No end of painted toe nails or flossed teeth or muscle can make a something without a human spirit or soul or mind into a human person.

You don't need a functioning brain to be human. Many people have defective and non functional brains. How much brain do you need and is brain the site of location of personhood? You can replace, amputate, remove any body part, and you are still the same person. You can even have a heart transplant and be the same person. How about a brain transplant? We haven't got there yet but it would seem that even then the intrinsic watermark of the original person into whom the new brain was put would shine through the new array of neuronal pathways and connections! Whatever about the person from whom the brain came, they would already have gone to their reward and their person or spirit or soul or mind would be long gone once their body was dead and their brain like their kidney would keep the new body alive. Like a second hand carburettor in a car. The brain is just a piece of software and it can function in any computer. The person does not travel with the brain always! If they die and stay intact the brain dies too. If they die and the brain is harvested and implanted in another human body it is just the brain and not the mind and soul that moves house. The recipient of the new brain just customises it to what it wants for it to do.

Body parts, brains, organic matter are all part of our makeup. They are a large essential part of the human being and flesh out (sorry) the person and personality. They are not the personality or the person. Person and personality are abstract or spiritual or idea level realities that live in human bodies and are dependent on human bodies to exist initially but which live on after the body or organic component decays and dies because they are immaterial realities and immaterial realities don't "die". They can be "relived" in film or verse or literature. They can be remembered and talked about. They can be described and profiled and filed away and be recovered and dusted down and continue to influence people. They are also alive in themselves (else for example how could they influence life once "dead"?) and presumably pine away waiting to be reunited with their beloved bodies like getting the band back together again. The natural state for the human mind/person/soul is for it to be united to a human body. We are not pure spirits and so we need our bodies and likewise our bodies need a person to inhabit them because without a person inside the body dies!

WHAT IS THE ESSSENCE OF MAN OR WOMAN?

Let's begin this heady consideration by seeing what you would harvest if you searched the internet trawling for philosophical thought on this topic over the past millennia. You would get trillions of hits and you would get an awful lot of thought! A very mixed bag of thought with divergent and contradictory ideas ranging from reincarnation, to animalism to materialism to existentialism to deism to pantheism to evolutionism to nihilism to rationalism to realism. Realism sounds good. Sometimes reading subway walls or graffiti is real and enlightening and the way to go. "I would prefer a bottle in front of me than a frontal lobotomy!" Deep stuff! "What goes up must come down". Wrong! I saw the film Gravity with Sandra Bullock and George Clooney and most of the stuff that went up didn't come down. OK I hear some experts say that in time it is all sucked into the earth's gravity or some other gravity and does come down somewhere. Fine! This film if you can hack it captures a man and a woman all alone in space. A good place to begin our topic. It is a surreal world of human isolation and loneliness floating around space between life and death. Everyone dies except Sandra. George goes to his reward by his own hand ......giving his life for Sandra who was tethered to him by a cord which could have done for both of them. Riveting display and I don't know what it is like in 3D but in 2D the human pathos and emotion are palpable.

This film and many other life situations dazzle us and rivet our attention through our identification with the protagonists. They are the same as us. They are human. It could be me! If it was a film about monkeys or dogs in space it could capture us but not in the same personal and close way. We can identify with the "personalities" of the animals and we can form attachments and take their sides but it is a little more distant than when it is with men and women. We become George we become Sandra and experience their emotion and fear and joy and perplexity. What do you do with your head, when like George after he has cut loose, you drift in space in your own little suit and helmet for ever .....until you die of whatever? Do you distract yourself if you can with thoughts or memories or words of country and western songs (as often wafts through this movie)? Do you die of panic? Do you struggle and hope for a way out? Ask George what he did!

When Sandra was all alone with everyone else dead in the Soviet Soyuz module, with no fuel and no where to go, and all day to go there, she had a moment. She shared her inner world with us and said she would pray if she knew how. She turned down the lights and switched off various panels and I think she was offloading oxygen and stay alive material when a space visitor came knocking on her window. It's George! He had seemingly made his way back from the frontiers of the next world, and his eternal float through space, to play an encore. He shows her how to use landing rockets to launch the Soyuz and then he disappears. The two most dramatic and soul exposing moments in any human life are caught in slow motion. The moment you sacrifice yourself for the life of another which is the same as martyrdom (George), and the zoning in of one's mind on the ultimate moments of one's life (Sandra) fast approaching. What do Sandra and George do and how do they react and …..how do we react? As you live so shall you die. There are no mystical experiences. There are no death bed conversions (usually unless it was brewing for a long time beforehand). There are no appearances of George Clooney to show us how to get out of it! This is it!

This experience is common. Most people with serious illness live with the prospect of imminent death every day. Most people going for risky life saving surgery or procedures confront death. Some see it as a break from their suffering. This is a complete turn around in the usual view of death. Instead of causing paralysing fear, they welcome it a comforting friend. It is still the same thing, death, so someone must be getting something wrong. What is the essence of man and woman? What is a person? What is personality? The answers to these thought provoking questions may cast some light on these different attitudes to the reality of death.

The first thing we experience as persons is our inner world. We are alone. We have a honing spot in our deepest selves. This is inviolable untouchable and free. The location of this self consciousness and awareness and sounding board is unknown. In the fourth stage of sleep or in any stage for that matter we lose conscious control of it. It is in safe hands because when we awake there it is smack bang in our minds and yes, it is me again! Welcome to another day! We have not changed overnight into someone else. We are the same and our memory is rebooted and our brain is awoken and our personality is spruced up for another day in the life of ourselves. During sleep, during anaesthesia, during dementia and during all out of mind and out of body episodes someone else must be holding the remote to our story, and giving it to us to restart "play" when we awake. We are the same guy in every conscious state but we often don't remember it. Sometimes we do and we remember vivid dreams and nightmares and visitations we had whilst asleep or in some other conscious state.

People do and can have a complete "personality change". Hopefully this is for the better. They can be toying around for a long time with the idea of quitting a way of life and starting off again brand new. This is usually good provided it doesn't mean reneging on vouched for responsibilities and obligations. People can undergo bad personality change following influence by bad atmospheres (getting involved in the drug world, beginning drinking with a group, opting out and living off the state etc). People can be so traumatised by an event or setback that they "take to the bed" or become withdrawn, or decide never to trust anyone again, or lose their joy. These responses can be due to a mental illness such as depression and may be amenable to counselling or psychotherapy. Other times these personality changes are permanent.

We do make and can make life long commitments. These are now part of our persons. They are what we do or where we live or whom we love. They are non negotiable. We gave our word. We *can* give our word. We can freely say yes or no. This could be the essence of a person. It is the state of really being free. We have a whole array of instincts and drives and passions and influences and thoughts and past experience and hopes but in our core, in our centre control panel we are free. We can do what we like. Really! We often don't do what we like because of what the neighbours would say or because we would suffer as a result or because it would be dangerous. But we can. The absolute kernel of the human spirit is based on and built on freedom. I do something because I want to. No pressure, no coercion, no strings attached. This is beyond thought. This is a mystery. Inside we are always free. If this is denied then it is a denial of personhood. In this sense we are not on pre-planned routes we are not programmed Google cars we drive where we want.

Everyone is subject to constraints on personal freedom due to the human condition, living conditions and responsibilities and obligations freely signed up to among other things. Freedom also has the idea of personal responsibility tagged on as a sine qua non. Freedom has consequences. We are not stupid (most of the time). We know there is no such thing as a free lunch. We know that actions have consequences. We know how life works. "Do you take this man/woman to be your lawfully wedded husband/wife?" This question and its answer imply total freedom to say yes or no. Lack of freedom would invalidate the vow. Here the totality, singularity, freedom and will or consent of a person are in action. The independence and totality and freedom of a real thing i.e. a human person, enacts the power of freedom in action. It is the will anticipating and encompassing all foreseen and unforeseen issues resulting from the free decision and saying yes. Underpinning all of the activity of the will and its freedom is love. A human being can love. The purest and best and ultimately only use and object of freedom is to show and express and enact love. That is really why we are free. We don't go through life with awesome "will I? won't I?" decisions on our minds all the time. We do have make or break moments when we have to make big decisions. Nothing and nobody can take our freedom from us. We can interiorly adhere to anything we like to all of the time. This may cost our lives, this may and does cost effort and suffering, and could cause ostracization and persecution and joy, because we are being true to ourselves despite all the pressure and temptations and human considerations. When the famous Greek philosopher Socrates had to drink hemlock because of his views, he did so freely because he knew his own mind and what he believed in and was not going to recant. When Thomas More was sentenced to death in the Tower of London he didn't think twice about whether he should obey King Henry VIII or God. He said he was "the King's good servant but God's first". When a child comes close to death a parent usually doesn't think twice about donating a kidney or whatever is needed to keep him alive. These and decisions like these are free, and motivated by love. This is the essence of being a person.

Love hurts, life crushes and there is no gain without pain. Our free decisions cost. There is a price for having deep convictions and strongly held views. We can hold things dearly. We can die for a cause. We value some things more than we value our own lives. That means there are things of more value than our individual lives. We are not the ultimate goal or rule of everything. We are very vulnerable and dispensable. We have however the seeds of greatness in our beings. The growth of this seed and the flourishing of our real worth and nature depend on our freedom. We decide. That is an essential characteristic of being a person. A person is a single piece of independent reality with possibilities determined by its freedom. We are born into freedom. It comes with us in our make up. Along with it comes the user's manual that tells us how it works. Then we get the book of life with all the possibilities of what you can do. Then when we reach the age of 7 we get the booklet of right and wrong. Later we get the handbook of responsibility. We are then fully equipped to choose. Our life ultimately is a mystery tour of free choices. It has the guiding star of love as the best route. It has cul de sacs and ravines and twists and hills to overcome and avoid. We have a fixed time frame to reach home and like monopoly we can gather money and points on the way or we can go to jail. We can be disqualified for ever.

Why would you do what you do? Why would you freely choose to give up your life for a cause, a person, a belief? How could there be for you, as a person, anything more valuable than your life? Your life is all you have and if you give that away for something else you must think the other thing is more valuable and important than your life. Your inner being and your wiring system know that there are seriously more important things than yourself and your life. Your loyalty to yourself and your person is more important than life itself. This is true because millions have given their lives for a higher cause. This is innate in human behaviour and in human love. We are not "what it is all about". There are perennial truths values and laws that cannot change, that are set in place somewhere else by someone bigger than us. There is a truth in life and in all that exists that we are also beholden to obey and respect and live by. It is not a cold clinical rule. It is overshadowed by Love.

The fact that people sacrifice their lives for a principle or a belief or a cause means that they hold their integrity and probity as persons or individuals more in regard than their earthly existence. This is a powerful endorsement of the value of honesty and our conscience. It promotes our freedom and our will and our motivation which is inspired by our love to the position of number one in importance in our lives. We never give up our lives for hate or for indifference. We can be tempted to give up or take our lives when we are overwhelmed and we see no way out of our misery. Self killing is motivated by an incorrectly understood and felt self love. We love ourselves and we want to stop the pain. This often is in the context of hopelessness. Lack of hope can be due to a mental illness like severe depression which can be treated. It can also be due to a world view, when a person judges that there is no more to life than what we live in the body and that there is no hope of another life. This is truly an existential nihilistic delusion. People have freedom being persons and people do end it all in full consciousness because that's all there is to life according to them. This is a disaster and failure in life. The pain can get so bad. The suffering can be so intense the disappointment can be so emptying that a person who believes in an afterlife and in God can also wish for death. Can wish it was all over. This floundering blind and confusing state calls out for relief. It calls out to all that designed and sustains this life to listen. To hear the cries of the just. To answer. Depth to depth cries out and the will to live is gone so what can you do? You have put all your eggs in the basket of freedom and personal choice and personal responsibility and life has dealt you a hand of jokers. What is left? What is there to do? What is the bottom line? The essence of the person knows love and has followed its path and now hopes in its saving hand, and this is sure. We are coherent understandable creatures. We understand pain and suffering and have loved and now when we are as low as we can go hope steps in and sustains us to persevere in the love we have always tried to live. This is truly the crucible of where the essence of a person is exposed.

The adherence of one person to the law and truth of life is worth everything. Culpable guilt, mitigated guilt, forgiven guilt from wrong doing are all out there. We feel guilt (if we are lucky). Those that never feel guilt are non existent. They can suppress it ignore it deny it and wall it off but it is there as a warning light to alert a person to something being wrong. We are born into guilt. We never wrote a book about it or read a "do it yourself" manual on it but we found it in our nature. It's innate it's just there. What is guilt? What is shame? They really affect us. They really are powerful stimuli to reconsider why we feel them. We can and do erase them and still live on. They are built for a purpose because everything in life has a purpose. They are not time expired prehistoric feelings because they are an intrinsic part of how a person works and if they disappeared a person could not function. They are warning lights in the cockpit that something is wrong. Our will can and does override them. This is our free choice. They are true feelings and emanate from our concept of fair play and right and wrong and also from what is objectively right and wrong. It's not just us. We have to lock on to the laws of nature and the universe and not vice versa. We also have to lock on to the laws governing mankind. We function as free agents but we happen to be living on planet earth with many others and how we relate to them and to ourselves and the planet are not of our making.

Obeying legitimate laws and rules and morals means we respect our vision and our freedom. We consider a shorter honest and truthful life better than a longer deceitful one. We judge that to be untrue to ourselves and our freely made decisions would be making our very lives and persons into fake stuff. It would make our person a counterfeit. We know this not so much through reasoning but by witnessing the actual happening and action we do when we are forced to choose. We have a long history in the world of various types of traitor. In Ireland they were called the "crowd that took the soup". They were traitors to their beliefs. This is a very strong word. It denotes a person who turns his back on a friend, a love, a being he owes loyaly to. We are all traitors in many things. We fall and fail and give in but usually we realise it and repent and make up and may even grow stronger in our support and allegiance to what it is we denied. In war a traitor endangers the lives of his comrades and country. In a job a traitor abuses his power causing damage to others. In marriage a traitor cheats on the other. Many treacheries are small but unless corrected they can become serious and even fatal. Some treacheries are by definition fatal. Court martial. Keel hauling. Hanging drawing and quartering all happened to traitors. These occasions to betray exist in life and why that is so is a mystery. It may be a testing ground for the truth of a person. It is the question "how much would it take to get you to do it?" Once you begin to negotiate you have conceded that you would betray, you would drink the soup, you would desert. This is a really sad occurrence. This is the defining point, this is the testing of the worth of a man or woman. Are you a person of your word?

A person's signature is as good as it gets legally. You sign on the dotted line. You *can* sign in the sense that it actually means something, it means you put your person on the line and you are free to do so. It puts your personal identity on the line. It identifies "you" with whatever you sign. This "you" is the totality of what a person entails. It is a bit of human nature in the shape of a human body with the functions of a human mind or brain which is self directing, loving, free, has a will and is self determinate. Is a baby a person? Like a baby hippopotamus is a small immature hippo, a human baby is a small immature person. It is a person. It will be a fully mature person given time. A foetus is the same. It is an immature person and like a seed in the furrow all it needs is water and warmth and nourishment and it will be a tree or a man or woman.

The essence of man is a living human being, with a present life and a potential eternal life. If you don't say this you deny an essential characteristic of being a person. A person has the potential and all the behaviours and signs of a being destined to live forever. That is a person in its full description. Anything less than this full description would cause a defect in the understanding and reality of the essence of man or woman much like a Japanese Bonsai tree is only a miniature of the fully mature tree.

Having stressed the importance of freedom for the essence of man, is it not love that is man's hallmark? The answer is of course yes. Love is the essence of man and woman but without freedom love is impossible. Freedom sets up and enables a person to love. The real heart of a person is their capacity to give and receive love. This is also the potency to be united to others in a bond of love. Ultimately to become one with them and even with the source of all love. You don't see this in any other creature on earth. Foxes don't chat up chickens. Sharks don't protect small fish. Donkeys don't let other donkeys down to the water hole first. Humans do. We are much more than rational animals. We are lovers. Persons essentially are individual free autonomous bits of love. This love matures and spreads and persons become more community and unity with time. A person has identity. This is Pat or Molly. But they still could be high functioning animals, rational but animals. Higher than a rational animal is a loving rational animal. Higher still is a loving rational animal with spiritual potential and a spiritual life and prospects. The pinnacle of what a person is, is a rational animal, who loves and receives love freely and who has the faculties to engage in a spiritual existence which is ultimately and eventually fulfilled in coming to know and love the personification of love i.e. in knowing and loving God Who is pure actualised Love.

THE CONVEYOR BELT

"What if God were one of us, just a slob like one of us, just a stranger on the bus, trying to make his way home." These lyrics from the hit song by Joan Osborne which made it to number one in some countries, really uncover the wonder of make believe…..the key verb being *believe*. They are arresting in their simplicity and powerful in their impact. Imagine! Some say they are true. The Catholic Faith says that God actually became man. This is it. Other religions are less specific. This datum changes everything and is the key to everything. Man and woman have been chatting and talking and thinking and wondering for years about everything, and here in the letterbox drops the key that answers all the questions.

The reason the world hasn't stopped and that journals and papers still churn out philosophy and psychology and human advancement is for the simple fact that we are primed and programmed to do this, because it is in our nature. People who accept that God became man also have day jobs and research and have problems and unanswered questions (of a lesser sort). God has not forcefully stepped in and said "Hey there stop everything".

Why not? When the owner of the restaurant comes in, or the boss visits the plant, the reaction is usually to stop everything and listen and pay attention and respect. After he goes you work even harder maybe, with a bonus or encouragement or new energy, or out of fear. When God came to visit his patch what happened? Well nothing! There were 12 followers who gave up everything to spread the news and 72 hangers on, and people came in droves to be taught and cured……..but overall things went on as usual. This must mean that God approves and knows what we are doing and just dropped in to say hello. The fact that a new human era did not occur (Did it not? Yes it did!) and that life was the same before and after, is surprising. It suggests that God wants us to keep doing what we are doing. That is of course looking at things from the outside, and not knowing what he actually said and did. It is like having a drone over Jerusalem with a camera observing God and the fallout of his visit. Answer? Nothing much to report. No war. No earthquake. No dishing out of money. The whole thing peters (sorry) out in his awful death on a cross. It couldn't have been God they report. No report in the New York Times. No newsflash. No tweets. No Google search data. It never happened. Amazing! Even more remarkable than the fact that God became man. He came and went and very few realised it. He allowed himself to be insulted, assaulted, pursued with hatred, crucified. Stop and think! If this were truly God we really have gotten things awfully wrong. This is shattering and tremendous. This is mind blowing and resets all our controls. We got it absolutely and completely wrong. We think the big drive is for power and wealth and success and notoriety.... and we never ever would have thought...this.

Such is life. Meantime we get back to routine and act as if it never happened. Like the Queen of England visiting Dublin last year. She came, and every news station was peppered with the news. She went, and we listened and we forgot what she said and we got back to normality. We are on automatic pilot and unless a whole opens up in the ground and swallows us like the sink holes that gobble up houses and cars in California, we just keep on going. We can disengage brain and unplug our minds from almost anything. To get our attention enduringly it nearly has to be chronic and serious....but even then you get used to anything, even pain. This is a powerful impulse in our lives, this urge that the show must go on. It is fantastic from the point of view that it disallows us from copping out (almost) and chilling out on-goingly (unless we are regular dope users or coppers out). The human mind and will is always "on". It does go to sleep of course usually at night but life forces it to make decisions and choices, and to live.

Newsflashes, like an earthquake somewhere, or a lotto win somewhere, or God becoming man, are just blips on our screen. We get supper and walk the dog and phone the family and carry on. Scary! The entire planet is just doing it! Like line dancing; the entire cosmos is advancing to the rhythm of life and some fall over the edge, like off a conveyor belt, and new stuff (humans, trees, frogs...) is put on the other end, and it all just moves along continuously and uninterruptedly. The sequence of the waves and the drifting of the clouds and the swaying of the corn and the chirp of the chipmunk, all sing in harmony towards the precipice, and this roller coaster of life .....never ends? It never ends just yet, in a generic way. For the individual chipmunks it does end in 2 years, humans 70 years, tadpoles 20 days... but the idea and reality of generic tadpole lives on! You will always find tadpoles on the conveyor belt of life!

So you have man and woman doing their thing, and wars and tornadoes and famines coming and going and what's left of man and woman after these disasters have gone picks itself up and lives again. They marry and are given in marriage and plant and reap and booom! They are swept away individually or in groups by accidents, illnesses, disasters....and those left behind just dust themselves down again and get back to normal again. What does that mean? Are they deaf? Are they impervious? Are they on automatic pilot? They are like wound up toys that cannot stop and take a change of direction. What needs to happen to wake man up? This is a really powerful onward march of humanity and it must be advancing somewhere. It is like and aging conveyor belt. You start young and then fall off when you are old (usually, though some tumble off when young).

What would the maker of the belt need to do to alert man, that look………"YOOUU HOOOO! Look at me …Here I am over heeere"! But no, man and beast are mesmerized and zombified into their formal march, and they don't know why and they don't know where. They don't know where the conveyor belt came from and who made it and why. What's the plan? A conveyor belt of life advancing always and constantly towards decay and death and falling off. All change is to decay in this world, overall. Bits and pieces of temporary newness in animals and humans and living things occur, but the machine inexorably drives life to death, one direction only. It never reverses. You don't get younger and neither do trees and elephants. Everything that exists gets old and dies.

The owner of the belt could say: "I made this belt and those folk, and do you think they stop to think about that? I keep giving them hints, like scaring them with sudden death storms, accidents and you might as well be talking to the wall. My warehouses are full of dead humans and cats and zebras and hills. Is there anyone that thinks at all? What kind of thing have I made? I will blow it all away with a deluge (and He did and only Noah and two of each species survived!). He then said enough of that, and I won't do it again and to prove it I will put my bow in the clouds. I'm at my wits end with this crowd! This is their last chance I will send my Son and get Him to talk some sense to them." And He did. And it's as if it never happened (??). We had our last best chance and the conveyor belt is trundling along and bodies and teeming life is falling off into the abyss and new stuff is being dumped on at the feeder end….and what's next, and we never even knew He came?

Does this go on forever? Does the belt crash and stop? Does it go into reverse and all the dead come back to life? How do you understand it? Well you could ask the owner. You could read his handbook (Gospel). You could engage brain and realise that there is more to this than "evolution". A funeral march of all that exists constantly dying and being replaced with new stuff. Evolution does not answer the question of how it all got started. How does it keep going? Why is it happening? Who designed it and all there is? What happens when you die? And the ton of unanswered questions about man and his nature and struggles.

God becomes man. Let's zone in on this fact. This is the holy grail of everything. This happened. The result was that many believed and accepted this reality. They changed their lives. They now lived according to a very demanding ethic and moral code and worshipped and loved God and believed in Him and hoped in Him. This caught on and has transformed the world. Wherever this belief went civilisation and education and the human tone and level increased and were perfected. People were happy. That is those who were true believers and practitioners of this code. The rest didn't believe and carried on as usual.

What is characteristic of believers? The major change is that they believe in a God they know. Up to this they were ordinary hardworking simple folk and when God came they welcomed Him and accepted and loved Him. Lucky them! Many didn't and still don't. What is the difference between believers and non-believers? It is a mystery. When a beautiful woman walks into the room and 10 lads look up, who would not jump up if she called him? God walks in and calls them by name and only one or two jump up and go to Him. Are the others blind and deaf and stupid that they don't recognise Him, and don't realise that "hey this your lucky day"? It has to be a mystery. Plainly said, when God created man He could have made us all "yes men". He didn't. Proof is that many are "no men" they don't believe in God. Is this strange? This is God's way. You have to seek God out to recognise Him. Most of His compatriots did not recognise who He was. You have to want to seek Him and know Him and listen to Him. He then communicates to you.

You may or may not like what He says to you. He may want a sacrifice from you. Give up women. Give up drink. Give alms. Love your husband better. Pray daily…. Some folk don't want the full package. They say God is OK but this moral law stuff I don't buy. God does not do part timers. It's all or nothing. Or at least strive to give all to Him. The will to want to accept and believe God and to do what He says or asks is crucial.

You don't have to be a believer to follow this story, but ease up and let it roll and see what happens. The idea of God becoming man is a good story line, and let it play out and put yourself in the frame and absorb the story. It is as good as it gets as regards this world, and when you allow it to seep into your mind and heart, is it not fantastic and heart stopping? How God thinks is a mystery. How we think is a mystery. How we think God thinks is beyond us (actually!). We are made in the image and likeness of God and have a quid divinum (something divine) which is our ticket into the world of God. God allows us to talk to Him, to listen to Him, and to act like Him. He even tolerates our studying Him and watching how he acts and speaks….and thinks. But God's ways are not our ways and life involves a meeting of minds: God's and ours, and guess who shapes whose mind? We become like God!

Other religions have other takes on God. Some are monotheistic (one God) and some are not (multiple gods) and some say He is a Person like us and some don't. Alcoholics ask help from a "higher power" and people in distress cry "God if you are there help me". Children pray to Holy God and their parents yell out "Sweet Jesus" when the child breaks the china vase. People in the throes of pain and agony and death rattles what do they do? They do what they always did. If God was their friend in life they invoke his kind help at this difficult time. If God was a stranger in life what do you know he is also a stranger at death. It is not as clear as all that because many people befriend God in ways they don't maybe realise and he is generous in returning any good deed and will come to their rescue.

The conveyor belt is now trundling to the precipice and Tommy has his last few Guinness and sees the headlights of the afterlife blazing his way and what does he do? What does anyone do? What do you do? Run like hell (sorry) to the doctor for another futile blast of chemo? Refuse to make a will! Ignore it. Get drunk! Cruise nonchalantly in your delusion toward a vacuum? Abandon yourself to the mercy of the living God? Make your peace with enemy and friend and God. Adhere to what sustained you throughout life and what you bought into with your free actions and way of living. That's what people do. They do what they always did. As you live so shall you die. But Tommy hasn't the energy to do any of that so he drifts calmly off the belt presumably having seen this day and prepared for it in the years and months before it. As you live so shall you die.

LOVE

"All you need is love …do di doo di do di do……" sang the Beatles. "Love hurts, love is a ring of fire, love is in the air, love is all you need." These are all key lines from popular songs. Is there a theme in music as sung about, a subject matter in literature as written about, or a whirlwind as powerful in life that comes even close to the hem of love's garment? It is a powerhouse of life and a lever that can move the earth. Love is not as much about cognition as about doing. Action speaks louder than words and behaviour is a more reliable indicator of thought and attitude than speech is. Love is beyond thought, it is operates at a much deeper level. It is the fulcrum of the person freely moving toward the beloved. It is a person gathering themselves up and giving themselves to another or to a worthy cause, freely and completely. In essence it is the desire to and the actualisation of total self-giving. It incorporates all the faculties a person has: thought, feelings, drives, hopes and fears, possibilities and baggage. It is the furniture removal truck carrying all the family's belongings and bringing them to a new house.

A key feature of love is its totality. This "no reservations mind set" taps into the power house we all have, and which is typified by expressions such as "love conquers, love will find a way, love can move mountains," which are also lyrics from songs. This avalanche or tornado that sweeps the human heart into action, and into whatever new way of living that is required, is our most powerful and beautiful attribute. It invigorates and energises a person and sustains them for the long haul. It is demanding and exclusive and permanent. In order to be called love it requires these characteristics. A half-baked temporary love is more like an infatuation, or a selfish love of oneself, or maybe a failed love, or an incomplete love. It isn't the brand version of love.

A genuine love never fails. A love can fall and can betray and can tire but it renews, if it is true. It becomes purified and even grows stronger with the amended knowledge and experience of its weakness. The faculty to love is true. We are not constructed with dodgy faculties, like some merchandise with the designer logo but made of counterfeit material. Our make-up is authentic. If not, we would be confused and anomalous like headless chickens running around a farm yard. We would be all over the place (beheaded chickens do run all over the place and it does look awful!) and we would not be able to bank on the truth or reality of our instincts or humanity. This would be a contradiction in our very nature. Apart from the speciousness of such a proposition, we have the witness of generations of people who have shown us that, yes, we are what it says on the tin. We are authentic and our nature is true and our instincts and rationality and drives and passions are intrinsically true…provided we accept human limitation and weakness and tendency to make mistakes …and then to acknowledge these faults and regroup and repair the damage. We fall but the lines are true and we can get back on line any time in life. There always is hope. There always is a remedy. There always is forgiveness. The expression "where there is life there is hope" is actually true.

Beyond the frontiers of human thought dwell love and hope and belief. Human thought is a meshwork of algebra or computer language that can and does profoundly affect us and our minds and our lives. But as they say, it's just talk. It does inform our mind-set and does focus our vision, but even without talk and words and thought we can and do function. A warm embrace, a cold shoulder, a feeling of loneliness and isolation, speak louder and more deeply to our being and person than clinical ideas. Yet ideas and thoughts and speech are the usual substrate that impact on us and contribute to shaping our minds and directing our action. It is our head at work. Knowledge is all powerful in this sense. But when all the waffle is said and all the sweet-talking done we can and do react with terrible strength to express and follow through on what we "know" deep down. The heart kicks in. We have the capacity to replay what we hear and say and think, and what others say and do and think, and in our mind's eye to re-evaluate all of this, and to get a second opinion and to check it out if necessary to see if it is true, if it is what we really agree with or not. We need not be fooled. We have a sensor in the depths of our being that can and does blow the rubbish away if we really want it to.

When all is said and done "do you love me?" is the key moment. "Well then show it by…..doing this, or that etc." Love has gone through the preliminaries of the thought process and now it is action, and thought and assessment and cognition second the game plan of love. Thought is now the servant of love and it is there to help the love last and excel and be true. Love has jettisoned the rational perambulations and is in orbit attracted maybe by the sun (the object of its love) and powered by an altogether more radical and powerful and all-encompassing and deeper force. It is now harnessed by love and the attractive force of this love, pile-drives the person to achieve and accomplish feats and endeavours it never thought possible. Love unleashes a new strength and force which would lie dormant and unused were it not for this love. Love is characterised by courage and daring and endurance and sacrifice. It is man's most sublime faculty.

Why is this so? What is love? Do we all need to love and should we love more people or things all the time to use this faculty to the full? You could go through life twiddling your thumbs and taking it easy. You could opt out and smoke weed and let it all pass you by. You could take the easy way out. Most people want to give life a fair shot. They are up for it and for whatever comes their way (provided it is ok and they don't mind it!). Life then "is like a box of chocolates as my Ma used to say" so says Forest Gump in the movie "and you never know what is going to happen". It is lights on and roll it, and take one, and you just never know…Life has all the deck and it dishes out various hands to different people. You meet a girl, you meet a boy, you get a job you take on responsibilities and the die is cast. You now enter into fully mature, eyes wide open, life. It is an adventure film, not a comedy, and hopefully not a tragedy! It could be an epic but that is up to you.

Real life is beyond thought. It seeps and surges and swirls and drives to the tune of inspiration and crafted world views and matured `takes` on everything. The foundations of our lives are deep seated convictions and experiences and, yes, inspirations or gut feelings that we probably have tried and tested and found to be reliable and sure. We live deep down there in the depths of our being and we also connect with others at this level. For example, we just like her kinky smile and we fall in love…no reason; we just do. She sees his needs and his face and gets all woozy and just falls head over heels in love with him. No reason, just likes him and then loves him. Bingo. Boy we have this really responsive and reactive sweet spot in our depths that once it lines up with an attractive soul mate there is nothing that can stop the chain reaction we call love. Tornado, avalanche, terrible love. All powerful brooking of no obstacle getting between it and its beloved! Stand back!

"Meantime back at the ranch" the heat dies down and the surge peters low and the exhilaration factor burns out…and she says "Honey it's yur turn to feed the chickens" and he says "sue thing darl I luve feedin them critters"….This is farmyard love and it is the real deal and it is mellow and low key. It could be built to last and built to be built on and matured and deepened. This love actually begets. A love that does not beget something is non-creative and therefore not love. Love is creative it generates it expands it spreads. Love nearly has a life of its own (in fact it has). When two people really love they are like a nuclear plant. They radiate joy and light and acceptance and friendship and approachability and attraction. Others notice it and are drawn to it and admire the beauty of this real love and want to participate in some way in love…if this is what it is and does. "Love makes the world go round" is also a song line and captures the essence and maybe the truth of the power of love. How about saying love creates?

You could live a life without love; I suppose. You could isolate yourself and focus on number one - me. You could spend your life building up your name, your prestige, your ego. You would then die and people could ask "what the hell (ooops!) was that?" and you know, they would be right. It could be a meaningless fruitless existence. Most people do love. Most people do hope. Most people do believe. These ordinary lives are dancing way beyond the frontiers of thought, and are growing in love and are founded on real sources of inspiration and energy and guidance called belief and hope. These guide-wires and stepping stones enable people to climb the summits of genuine life and true love. They are real beacons and stimulants toward the pinnacle of human existence. Everything else pales when compared to the quality and calibre and sublimity of their quest and ultimate accomplishment. It is truly living on the edge of human thought and yet is more solid and robust than all the world of ideas.

Your mother told you never to eat raw plums. Your Da told you never to go into that public house. Your boss told you never to divulge your password. These and the myriads of other advices we get are based on trust and belief, that the person we know and trust, knows more than we do and so we put trust in their word, and hope it all turns out well. This behaviour is not based on our cognition but on our trust and hope. Taken to a higher and broader level this is where the real drama of our lives is based. We forge our thoughts and weld our behaviour patterns and skewer our vision so that we expurgate the dross from our minds and souls and lives, and strengthen the bulwarks of our personalities, mostly based on our trust in what others tell us, or on our experience of life or on inspiration we get. When all of the advice we get is good and true and we believe it and act on it we are on a winner. Our true lives are more in the blacksmith's forge than in the thought chamber. When all the thinking is done and you get a toothache, or the car gets a flat tyre, or the fire alarm goes off, you have to act and "get real". Real nitty-gritty life doesn't do fancy thought. It does graft and effort and application of our whole being and person to concrete tasks and not to "philosophy". This is a bit unfair because we do have to think and work things out and formulate a mental backdrop of understanding of life and flat tyres and broken toe nails. But whether we have a deep understanding of the warp and woof of daily life or not the show goes on and we are forced to act. Taking advice from others is essential for living because without this we would have to prove everything to ourselves and this is impossible and stupid. To get up to speed with life we build on others experience and knowledge. In educational institutes this is usually tried and tested and reliable knowledge and excellent graduates are the result.

You have to use your entire brain and mind ....brain stem, cerebellum, frontal and posterior lobes and limbic system and whatever else is in the bag. All of it has to engage full on in life and not just the inferior frontal gyrus of the dominant frontal lobe (speech area of Broca!). The frontal lobes and intellectual lobes are crucial and can make or break us, by feeding the rest of our brain/mind with good solid true thought or with dodgy unfounded garbage which could send us in either the right or wrong direction. But once it has set the scene the intellect is tagged on behind the roller coaster of belief, love and hope which drive our carriage through the new worlds of really human life. We are not computers or hand held devices "companions for life type of gismos." We have a body and feelings and hurts and joys and forgiveness and guilt and a future and we die. A computer may be smarter than we are at preloaded cognitive data but it sure can't down a frothy beer or caress a beautiful woman. Now that is beyond thought! And that is real life.

What is the well spring of our thoughts and desires and hopes? There must be some source. Everything we know has a cause and everything we know has a purpose. Why wouldn't you probe the depths of what you or we all think and dream to see why on earth we think and dream the things we do? Is it hardwired into our nature? Is it like the software we get with a new computer that allows the machine to work on Apple or Microsoft or whatever? Are our intuitions correct and can they tell us about ourselves? The associations we make and the conclusions we come to, we possibly don't understand them, but perhaps we feel them and maybe they are true. Yes they are generic and we all experience them and they are also tailor made for each individual, and unless wilfully or inadvertently interfered with to cause malfunction, they are true and real.

"And the lights all went out in Massachusetts" in the famous song by The Bee Gees relates to the light of their love going out. A bit of a long shot you may say? To a certain extent the lights went out for him because that was the way he felt after "leaving her standing there". Love had died and so had a vision and experience and a light in his life. This is also the story in a broader and more lasting way when we fail in love long term. It also occurs when a dear friend or spouse or relative dies. A light goes out and we are inconsolable. A friend's death is not a failed love but a change in the circumstances of love. We have loved each other 'til the end and the human contact and consolation is now gone and something else lives on. The love lives on in memory and recollection and intention. With a failed love this does not happen. It disappears and leaves a void. Our vision is constricted and our joy and zest for life somehow dwindle. We always have the capacity to light up again though and hope keeps us buoyed up.

Hope breathes eternal and that must mean something. When there is love in your life it is all worthwhile. Without love it is hard to live.

How could you live without love? Love is the driver. Love is a spectrum. It goes from small loves to gigantic loves. The small loves keep the home fires burning and can ignite into a conflagration if we want it to. Our love can be for ourselves and even though it is a shabby version of love, it still ticks the box and keeps the faculty from atrophying. This selfish love with time and circumstance can burst out of its egocentrism and reach out. It then can be called real love in the correct meaning of the term. Such a theme is depicted in Dickens "A Christmas Carol" where Scrooge bursts out of his miserly ways to reach out to others after the visitation of the ghosts of Christmases past.

Love changes everything. Pain and effort have meaning "he ain't heavy he is my brother". "Climb any mountain cross any sea to be with you" (U2 pop group). "I married Maureen and she got MS at 25 and I've nursed her 35 years." This is some life choice. This is some love but having said that, not unusual. What a phenomenal expression of enduring love. What is it? How do you explain this sublime behaviour affection and self sacrifice? It is a vision beyond pain and sacrifice. It is beyond pragmatic animal life. It is duty and loyalty and the pinnacle of the will's capacity on earth. It is the jewel in the crown of humanity. It is surpassing our own lives to give to another or to a good cause. It has the mark of transcendence in that it makes little sense in this life to some extent, and must be sourced and inspired and energised toward a superior goal. It does bear fruits of joy and affection and fulfilment in this life. But it is a mirror of something else. It is a reflection of a powerful magnet that generates and creates and sustains and moves everything. It involves a sacrifice of life for another or a higher goal. Its terms and conditions transcend this life. It is attractive contagious and does nothing but good.

Love resides in the will which is our most prized possession. It is stronger than death. It is an essential characteristic of true mature man. Generosity and having "a big heart" are prerequisites for enduring love. They are the forerunners and they develop and mature with loving. Without love death becomes a way to live! The description of true loves include: being humble loving and affectionate; long suffering; simple, in the good sense; grateful; good people to be with; bringers of peace and joy. When they die they are sorely missed and they leave legacies of joy and peace.

Love is a crafted effortful endeavour. Like a mother caring for her child, or a friend looking out for his pal, the job spec is open ended. Anything is possible and there is no effort too great. Great loves, like giving one's life for another, or dedicating one's life to another or to a family or to a good cause bespeak a generous spirit and a firm will and a whole hearted journey. It is much more difficult if even possible if one is half hearted or two minded or trying to renegotiate the contract. People are weak. People have good intentions, but as a friend from a communist country said to me "failure is not an option". He was speaking from experience. We really need to be single minded about what we are about. People *are* capable of this degree of commitment. A soldier in an elite group must be 110% committed or else they all could be killed. A team member should be full blooded about the team or else they will underperform. A Mount Everest climber has to be focussed and prepared and knowledgeable about the climb or else he will fail or die. We are able to do the big thing, we are able to achieve big targets, we are able to surpass ourselves. It is a combination of maturity, of not over or under-estimating the challenge and of having as much preparation as we can get, and then of going for it full on, whole hearted for as long as it takes. This will mean set-backs and tiredness and possibly illness and disappointments, but as the beginning of the TV series Mission Impossible used to say when the agent got the instruction tape: "this tape will self-destruct in 5 seconds, good luck Dan." After that it was action all the way and they always came out tops. This is not love but it is a good image for perseverance and total commitment, essential characteristics of love.

Sometimes you may not know what a thing is but you can deduce its nature by its effects. The key effect of love is happiness. It brings peace, sometimes at the cost of war because it is loyal to its principles, but it spreads joy and peace. There is no real love that does not have this effect. It keeps the person true. They may fall and make mistakes, which are inevitable but they always recoup and maybe apologise and get going again. Love is a lifelong project. You don't retire. You don't slacken off. You get even better at love and become more intense and committed as the years go on. This is often in the face of even more difficult challenges and trials as one gets older. Why do lovers say "I will love you for ever"? They mean it. It is expressed with their entire being and full sincerity and this is the backbone of all genuine human life. A life without love is a paradox. It is almost meaningless.

Is loving yourself, love? In the correct sense of loving, what is good for oneself whilst fulfilling obligations to others and society is love. But what is good for oneself? Our lives are lives of service. This aspect of being alive gives meaning and value to our lives and contributes to the wellbeing of others. A life of self imposed isolation, of selfish objectives, and self absorption and of seeing others only as means to progress our own ambitions is a very low form of existence. Of course worse than this is a life of crime and hate and revenge. Many live such depraved existences and are themselves very unhappy and they also make others unhappy. They are lonely creatures unloved by anyone including themselves. The real heroes are the ones who raise the level for themselves and others and excel at building up others and the community. They source their energy and altruism in their own world view and convictions. They have been loved. They have received gifts and as a consequence they want to act likewise. People who serve others, who love others also have strong self identity and personality and they adhere faithfully to a strict code of conduct for themselves. Many such people believe in God. They feel loved by God and endowed by everything they have from God. They want to act like that too and they give of themselves to others. They are happy to serve and look out for others and give little attention to themselves. They even forget about themselves. They are the freest of all men. They are not attached to themselves or of what they have or their name. Their locus of control is outside themselves. They are focussed on helping others 24/7.

Altruism is the secular version of this type of behaviour. People with loads of money try to give it to worthy causes. They help the poor. They contribute to eradicating illnesses. They set up foundations like Bill and Melinda Gates. Many people have a social conscience and give money for the poor. Others do voluntary work or free tuition or hours of work. These all come from the same stable as love, and the ultimate giving is when a person gives his very self, expecting nothing in return. Have we got what it takes to sacrifice ourselves to that degree? If so where does that faculty come from? It bespeaks another life. If all there is, is this one life we live, and after that nothing it doesn't make sense to blow it all away in giving it to others. We do have that desire and drive to actually give ourselves totally and it isn't an intellectual conviction but a deep seated desire and goodness. It is good it achieves good and it does good to the giver. Such goodness is not listed in the seven habits of successful people. It is not mentioned in the management courses. It is not covered in medical curricula or social science curricula. It is not pragmatic. It is not utilitarian. It doesn't advance you in this world or make you more money or even business contacts. It is outside the realm of usefulness as seen with worldly eyes. Yet it really is the oil that makes the engine turn smoothly. It is the glue holding society together. It is the glint in a person's eye and the joy upholding the lives of people. Take it out and we would all be in it for ourselves and all we could get and the world would be a cold uninviting place full of isolated lonely selfish people. It would disintegrate. Love keeps the world going around. It puts the smile on humanity and the affection and understanding into our lives. It is the only thing worthwhile when all is said and done.

We all have a seed of love in our beings. A human without love is ….dead. Everyone alive has at least the possibility of loving and of entering this cycle of love. Life essentially is all about love. It is the background music, it is the stage prop, it enlivens the script and it writes the screenplay. We are all lovers. We can't help it but we can grow in love or shrink it. Our free choices and effort to struggle to love are what we spend our lives doing. Love in this life is like preschool. It is an antecedent of pure love. It is very demanding and costly in effort but we see beyond the pain to the love. Love is essentially for another person. We cannot love a dog. We cannot love a house or a charity work as such. We love people. Love has as its object a person. We also receive love and not to be willing to be loved is also a defect in our love. It is marked in our nature that we love. We didn't put it there we were born with it in our being. We have a gut feeling it is good and right and we also feel we should love. Why? We also feel like not loving like hating like robbing like being unjust or unfaithful but we know it they are not right or good. Thus love demands effort to "do the right thing".

WORK

What is work? Is it just body language and the animal equivalent of foraging? For most people it is a necessity. It is a daily task, unattractive, tiring and necessary. Housewives of the world, farmers, industrial workers assembly line operatives. Blue, white, grey collar workers. Sweat shirt workers. Academics manual workers and artists. All have a common thread. Doing stuff. Service. Making a dollar. But what is it? It is a participation in the dynamic of "act".

The very fact of being alive means we are in action. Our heart beats 72 times a minute, mostly, our lungs expand and contract 14 times a minute and every little piece of our bodies is at it non stop. We are in perpetual motion. Our brains and minds are being perfused and nourished and renewed by the blood stream and immune system and other systems we hardly know about. We are ticking over like a well tuned engine. Work happens when this engine is harnessed to perform a directed task with a valuable purpose. It is a goal directed activity. It is meant to achieve something useful.

Useful can have varied meanings. It could be service to others, the community, the company or other worthy enterprise. It advances humanity in some way. All genuine work has this characteristic that it improves or supports or advances well being of humanity. If not it is not work in the true sense of the word. Aimless activity with no real purpose or goal could not be called work because it may have doubtful benefit to the doer and has no intrinsic value in itself. If nobody worked the place would fall to rack and ruin. The planet and all we know changes all the time. Nothing does not change. All change in the long term is toward chaos. A new baby or plant or car go through a process of maturation and development which seems to contradict the universal law of entropy (everything tends toward chaos) but age and decay they all do. Fleeting new things sprout up all the time. Life engenders new things constantly and like a conveyor belt heading toward a precipice they all inexorably trundle along and get old and fall of the end of the belt and die. They are all recycled and massaged into earth or matter of some basic description and who knows but they may participate in another adventure of some form of life…be it a baby or a shrimp or a plastic bottle. This is the great cycle of nature. Someone somewhere is turning the wheel of life and as long as he/she doesn't get tired the process goes on and on.

You could say that work re-establishes some order on proceedings. It causes order to happen and it also builds on the chaos. Work constructs the world mainly for man's benefit. Work also fulfils man's innate need to work. How about saying that man was made to work? How about saying that suitable lifelong work is good for man's physical and psychological and social and spiritual health? It's true as all research in the area repeatedly shows. Unemployment is a disaster for man. He is out of the loop. He is in poverty or just above poverty. He often will get disheartened and depressed. He may not fill his time well and can and does drink too much take drugs get involved in criminality and drops out of mainstream society. Studies of the effects of employment and unemployment on people are common and show that work is good for man. In UK these last months doctors are being encouraged to write fit for work certificates instead of sick certs. Unemployment and all it brings with it causes bad physical health bad mental health and bad financial health. Work sustains man gives him purpose and a reason to live and a status and money. It is fulfilling and gratifying to do a good job. It is rewarding and challenging to solve problems. It is a forum to meet new people and to forge friendships. What else would man do if he didn't work? The sick have as their job to get better. The unemployed have as their job to try and get a job, and meantime to plan their days and do voluntary work, or further learning, or reading, or coaching or something useful. The idea of sitting watching TV is a recipe for disaster. Work also reveals hidden functions and applications of matter which otherwise would not be either known or used. Without man and without work there would be no fibre optics or computers or cars or ....pollution! The pollution bit is a little unfair because the animal population of earth is in trillions when you count mammals, birds, fish, amphibians and they all have a carbon footprint. There are only 7 billion humans. The carbon pollution from manufacturing and power plants etc is an occasion for work, to see how it can be corrected and how production can be made carbon friendly. This is new information and advancement and is thanks to ongoing work. If it were not for man there would be no cars, no cd players no cigarettes. We discover hidden potentialities inherent but untapped in matter. We also fill the world with education and books and music and ideas. These are all highly ordered and even beautiful productions. We don't invent new ideas or things but we discover what is already there and what its potentials are.

Work also has a personal impact on the worker. Some say man was made to work and that he is healthiest and happiest when working. This is true. But what does work do to man? It forges behaviour control. It forges discipline. It keeps him out of mischief and gives him occupation and a role in life and in the community. It has social aspects and public aspects like: "Who is that? That's Mary from such and such a street, and she works in Cadburys. That's Tom the plasterer. That's Ronaldo the soccer player". Playing soccer is also work for professionals!

The decline and decay and disorder that is universal and affects everything we know, is in stark contrast to the astounding intricacy and detail and beauty and advanced nature of even a single cell, not to mention the galaxy or the human brain. How on…..earth??...did this awesome complexity which functions like clockwork ever get into the equation of inexorable action and progress to death and disorder and decay? How could an aging and rusting world give rise to a beautiful highly complex baby? This is a major show stopper. How when everything is getting worse do you get a new anything, and what's more a highly developed and advanced and living being or plant or rock pool? How does an acorn grow into an oak? This can't be nature in the observed fall and decline of everything model we see all the time. Despite the slow decline in everything we know over time, there seems to be a time capsule somewhere with a warehouse of new stuff that keeps brand new exhilarating beings and things coming out and walking planet earth for a few years, and then like the earth getting old and dying. Is it that when everything was first made it was all squeaky clean and new and it is all getting old and decrepit over time? If we replayed the last n years would everything get new again? Did it have a beginning date? If time is eternity how come it took 'til now to get to this stage? What was before time? Is time just a material thing? Is time a human thing? What is time? There are 2 processes going on all the time. On the one hand everything is slowly dying. On the other everything is being hatched and growing into maturity. Life sprouts from the earth from the seabed from living beings. Yet this exuberant power of new life has a best by date and it all withers away in time.

Are there reservoirs of tin and babies and plants in some warehouse deep in the cosmos? The planets and universe is an old man now and yet it produces shiny metal and succulent lamb and tender leaves. Is there a finite reservoir of new stuff housed in the universe and are we living on reserves which are finite and will be exhausted some day? Like the oil wells or water reservoirs? The total volume or mass or extent of the universe is fixed. This is so because out of nothing you can't make anything. You cannot create out of nothing and we are using up all the good stuff and soon (billenia of years?) we will have no new stuff left. The only way this roller coaster of new life and dying life can continue for ever is if someone creates out of nothing because the material is all getting very old and worn out. The source of life has not failed yet but what keeps it producing? What feeds it? Who designed it? Who drives it? What stops a sinkhole swallowing the whole universe up?

How do you get life out of death? How do you get new out of old? How do you get exquisite delicate detailed design and manufacture and function out of increasing chaos? How do you get extraordinary order out of extraordinary disorder? You throw a wastepaper basket full of rubbish on the floor and come back in 10, 20, one million minutes and….it is still there but even worse. How many millennia do you wait to get a new car or washing machine suddenly or not so suddenly popping out of a municipal dump? Who was the last guy to find a brand new Rolex watch in a swamp? (evolution!) You do not get new or designed anything from rubbish or from earth or from life as we know it. It has never happened. How about a pearl in a shell? Nice one. Well that is amazing but a pearl is sediment (nice sediment) that eventually also decays and deteriorates.

What is old? What is change? Why do things get old why do things change? Why don't things get younger and more fantastic all the time? Is new life just like a death rattle or fragile leaf growing on the trunk of a dying tree? Is the elephant breathing his last and are we just microbes under his nail? Is the show over and are we the terminal strains of a tragedy? In any wilderness or even garden you get disorder if you don't put order on it. You need to plant in lines with patterns to get any order in the garden or wilderness. In a kindergarten you will reap wild kids and absolute chaos unless you train and enforce discipline. "Someone" must establish order. Order is not natural from our observation and experience.

How about the cosmos and the sea and the orbits? Absolutely! "Who" put order on them? That is the question. We didn't because we are too small. A much bigger person must have done it. This macro sized order (of the universe) is also tending toward disorder as it is all expanding and being blown apart. Someone must have established order on everything to start with and ever since that it is all falling apart. "HE" had better come back and reset the order!

Our experience is that everything dies, everything tends to disorder, everything gets old. Our experience is that new life emerges all the time. This new life is squeaky new beautiful and highly complicated and designed. This design is not spontaneous. Nothing is spontaneous in life. How does new exhilaratingly complex life occur….without a superhuman intelligence doing it? It can't.

You cannot get life from death. (But, it is happening all the time. We can't do it and never have or will, but "someone" else is doing it all the time!). You cannot get order from disorder (but ordered things are cropping up all over the place, and we are not responsible for it). You cannot get young from old (but the world is full of young ones). Where do all the new, ordered, young things come from? The theatre props and the conveyor belt of life are toward aging and death and demise. Where is the source of brand new complicated life and beauty? Is there a white matter zone we don't see? Is there a reality of which we are unaware? Are we seeing the full picture? This emergence of new life from old bottles and rubbish is inexplicable. It should not be happening according to our evidence and experience of the patterns of life here. No one can explain how you get new life. Nothing happens in this life unless someone does it. It seems to us that humans are the only ones putting order on things. No one else is doing it. The animals have their own instinct and patterns (nest building) (migration) and yes that is against the disorder grain in nature. It could be said that the order humans and animals contribute is only a temporary blip and once the short time frame is elapsed the wheels of disorder and entropy take over again and chaos continues.

All permanent and long lasting change in the universe is toward degradation disorder and decay. There is nothing that does not change. Everything we know and see or experience gets old and decays with time. The present chaos in the climate and global temperature are stark examples of how change occurs. Everything changes because for one thing everything is temporary. There is nothing that will last forever. To last for ever means either it does not change or that it is perpetually renewing itself with an everlasting principle driving or powering it. The latter does not seem a credible option and we have no evidence of it. The solar system is in constant change with black spots on the sun and meteorites and falling stars and increasing distances from the sun. We change and die as do all living things. The inanimate things corrode and wear out and disappear. All change means temporality and decay. The world as we know it is passing away!

Man and his shovel undo some of this earthly decay and put order where it was not before. When you look at the impact that man has had on the continents over the last 500 years it is mainly toward order and advancement. He has harnessed the natural resources and made them produce tools and buildings and communication systems. He has studied plants and animals and made them suit his needs. He has written laws to govern peoples and composed music and literature and art to express himself and to entertain others and allow them to look beyond (this present life). He has exposed beauty in all the sense modalities to the benefit of mankind. All this is due to individuals working. Without work none of this would have happened. Work does not explain the tendency of the universe toward chaos and decay but it does temporarily arrest the decline in some areas at any rate. It goes against the tide of death and decline and decay. Work builds and mends and brings progress. It seems to be out of place in a dying planet. It seems to reflect another level of being. It definitely is action and activity. It definitely is ordered and has a goal or purpose. It helps the worker to have good health. It sustains man during his life and for a while it constructs an environment for man to live better. Imagine if all humans disappeared and the planet was left to the animals! Come back in 100 years and wilderness and wild beasts would inhabit earth. Work would not have happened for a century. The place would be in rack and ruin. So work is a human thing. The animals don't work if left alone. You do get working dogs and mules and horses but they are forced to do it. It is not their nature.

Why work? What is it? It is action. It is directed activity. It achieves something. It is part of the way we are. It is a participation in life. The whole universe is at it. Everything after its nature is doing its thing. The earth spins, the sun shines the donkey brays and man, what does man do? The verb here is the key: to do. He works. We are geared to do things. We sleep 8 hours a night usually and the other 16 hours are for doing things. I wonder if there is the pinnacle of "doing" anywhere? I wonder is there a better worker than man? I wonder what is the ultimate purpose of work? It does help man who does it as we have seen, but the value of action, rationally based action, is important in itself. Rationally directed action is of a higher level than animal based action. How about constant spiritual action is that even higher? How about pure act? What is that? That is constant sublime activity beyond our wildest dreams. It is like a computer's capacity to calibrate to infinity compared to our basic maths. It is Van Gough's Sunflower painting compared to a child's crayon drawing. It is the power of the sun compared to a candle. Action must have an ultimate cause and source. We buy into it for our lives but "it" continues with the world and all the living. When we die we stop work! We stop acting, our action renewal card has expired.

But in this life there is action, there is act. There is not inaction or stasis. In other words this life is all go. It is all about doing things. It is all about change and time. Time is not a substantial reality. Time is an accidental quality of change. No change, equals, no time. If everything was pure act. That would mean everything was in absolute action full throttle all the time which is "now". The only time would be now. Everything ever in the entire cosmos now. No change? Good question. What does all the action achieve or do. Well it does one thing we can see I think. We are….we are a new thing, we weren't always around and even the most hard nosed evolutionists would agree. So we are new. The universe is new also, it wasn't always there. So all the action of pure act creates for one thing. It loves for another. It knows for another. And it participates in its creations as we see in our realm. We don't hold the remote for life, pure act does. We have a bit of act but act itself calls the shots, makes the rules, calls us home, and creates more of us all the time …………..for the present anyhow. The CEO of the universe has a big job…all agree? Bigger than Bill Gates or Obama rolled into one! That demands a lot of action and knowledge and love, to sustain repair protect and guide the 7 billion of us in one branch of the company at present, and keep the universe on track. That's what I call work! Asking: Why work? Is like asking why earth exists or why birds sing. We do, that's it, so the real question is why and what does it mean. As we have tried to show, it all has to do with act or action, and possibly the higher the revs or intensity of action that we achieve the more perfect we are? Certainly a hard working person has more prestige and traction than a lazy good for nothing. This means work has value in our eyes and it is a "good" as such. Action is a good once it has the shape of work i.e. it is directed to a good for man and it is honest and a service to the community.

The other thing about work is the why. The reason a person works is also important. You could work to feather your own nest and everyone has to do this to the extent of making a decent living. But to work only for yourself and not to contribute to others is selfish. It could be an ego trip building up your own name for your own gloating purposes. This is taking the honour from work. Work done to survive to make a living, to help others, to contribute to society, to love….what? Yes love, is the best and highest motivation for work. To do it out of love. Love for one's wife or husband or family for ones relatives for the village for friends or neighbours. Our motivations to work are multiple but to elevate it to a loving action is a great goal. Mothers look after children and spouses out of love. Daughters look after mothers out of love. CEOs if they are good look after the employees out of, well, care and concern and fair play and because they like them …in a word love.

SURVIVAL

Take one: the key to survival is multifaceted. Take two: the key to survival is written in the stars. Take three: the key to survival is beyond our capabilities to a certain extent. It depends on chance, on serendipity ….on providence! An awful lot depends on what the challenge is and on what the resources are. To survive a football match, a diner party, a long hike, or life, you need a different skill set. Survival implies the idea of being alive after the encounter, whatever it may be. In normal life this usually depends on the basic skills or strengths of the person, anticipation of what may be in store and preparedness. To climb Everest wisdom is crucial since the ascent is strewn with the frozen bodies of wannabe climbers who just didn't make it. To know therefore when to quit on Everest is life or death stuff. All the preparation and the study and training, the weather forecasts and the team and the drive to succeed, are essential components for any serious attempt of reaching the summit. When everything is as good as can be, the last variable then enters the equation, and that is chance or luck or the hand of God. Anything from illness, to a fall, to an avalanche, to inclement weather, could all abort the climb or even cause death or injury. One has to have a plan B, a strategy of how to cope when route one fails. The Everest web site and adventurestats.com make sobering reading. 11,000 attempts have been made to climb Everest of which 3,000 reached the summit, which is a 29% success rate. The fatality rate is 2.05%, or 207 climbers, 54 of whom had reached the summit. Still want to climb?

If you are elderly and you fall and break a hip the chances of survival are 33% good, 33% never fully recover and 33% die. If you get one episode of depression the chances of getting a second are increased, and if you get two episodes the chances of getting a third are greatly increased. It is all to do with risk balancing, actuarial data on what has happened to millions before you, and luck. Without car insurance you might never crash and be alright. The insurance companies have done the sums and know the percentages. With insurance you can crash if you like and you will be financially covered! There is no insurance for life however, understood as a sure guarantee of always being safe. Life is unpredictable and you just never know. To get back to the car metaphor, you can reduce risk of accidents by having a road worthy car and by driving carefully and by anticipating what other drivers will do. You increase risk by doing the opposite. Even with all the precautions in place accidents do happen and you could be involved. There are no absolutely secure guarantees with driving either it seems. The issue of human error, circumstantial conditions out of one's control like the weather or lighting or distractions, and unforeseen events all come into play. The end result is that you give things your best shot, and prepare as best as you can, and then whatever happens, happens. The success and failure rates for various activities can have a consistent value, for example no matter how well prepared people are to climb Everest only 29% on average will make it to the top, and within this number those less well suited or prepared do even worse.

This seems all very bleak and sombre. However the success rates for most things we do are well into the nineties. Washing your hair 100% success! Feeding the dog 100% success! Getting a parking space 98% success and 100% with a parking charge! We are used to success in our daily lives and we may even follow a football team that always wins so we have more reasons to celebrate and feel good and have bragging rights. We like success. It keeps us going, and if it is a significant success and possibly hard won it is all the sweeter or better. It buoys up our hope gives us confidence and that winning feeling. It engenders the "can do" mentality much beloved of business gurus. The opposite - having strings of failures, can have a disheartening effect and can dull our zest and even cause depression. That is why it is important when dealing with children not to be too critical and corrective all the time, but to make sure they have encouragement and hope and therefore they keep trying. Otherwise they could just give up or become cynical and despondent. Most people don't climb Everest but most have significant challenges. With the recession in the Northern Hemisphere many are sorely tested to try to make ends meet. Hoards of young people have had to emigrate to get work. Millions have had to seriously reduce expenses and the numbers of homeless and destitute has rocketed.

The numbers of people on the peripheries of society worldwide is staggering. The shanty towns of big cities like Sao Paulo, Beijing or Mumbai, and the arid expanses of eastern Eritrea, southern Sudan or Congo are inhabited by millions of people who don't have the basic necessities of life. These people have survival as their second name and as a constant concern every day. There are estimated to be 9 million Syrian refugees, two and a half million have fled to other countries and six and a half million are internally displaced. This is a sample of the worldwide struggle for survival. The overall figure for people in serious need must be in the hundreds of millions. This gives some benchmark for the universal fight for survival and how it is of life and death proportions for large percentages of humanity.

The survival picture in the Western world is somewhat different. There it is not so much about food and water and shelter (though it often can be), but more to do with financial stress, illness, unemployment, peer pressure, old age, disability and so on. Surviving a difficult work situation, or a difficult relationship, or panic attacks or alcoholism can really tax one's coping skills. Often professional help is needed to tackle such issues. A person may be dogged by guilt, or morbid memories from past events, or by fears of what they don't know, and these can envelop a person's life. They cause real suffering and require survival or management strategies. Bullying either face to face or on the internet has caused many to become depressed and even take their own lives. Physical illness especially when chronic is very demanding and requires a special set of survival skills. It is more to do with managing the illness and oneself than about conquering it. Support groups and counsellors and psychologists help these people to cope long term.

Perceived slights or insults or general disengagement from life, has caused people to open fire with semi-automatic weapons in schools, shopping malls and colleges, with resulting death tolls of innocent people. All of the worst things that can happen in life, have already happened, and have usually had devastating outcomes. War wipes out generations of young men and families and destroys countries and infrastructure and costs a fortune in money and lives. It causes untold suffering and harrowing pain and grief. It is the worst of all the evils to be visited on man. America and EU have thousands of veterans who survived war. The percentage with post traumatic stress alone is 25% at a modest count. These are mainly young men in their 20's and 30's who have their whole lives ahead of them.

Is there a point beyond which you can't survive? Is there a breaking point for everyone? Is there always a tipping point? These are difficult questions because everyone is not the same and circumstances differ.

Let us answer by saying that there are people who have not broken when severely tested. Among these are the martyrs for various causes (legitimate non fanatical martyrs) who die rather than betray a principle, a person, a country etc. There are the ill who live on with their illness until they die from it. There are the myriads of people who live with adversity, how they don't know, and who survive. These and more testify to the existence of people who go the distance, who survived. It is not a shame to be afraid. Many people are afraid of illness, of adversaries, of embarrassment, of failure. The goal is to see what really needs to be done and to try and do it. This may require help from family friends and professionals, and it may mean accepting ambivalence and partial success while all the time focussing on survival and on overcoming the obstacles. It is not a shame to get sick or depressed or burnt out and then to get treatment and continue on.

In general it could be said that different people have different breaking points at which "they can't go on" and they become ill or decompensate in some way. A person who indulges a passion for guns may lose control and shoot up the place, and we unfortunately we have too many examples of this. A stalker may strike and assault the victim. A person harbouring hatred for another may suddenly or not so suddenly, kill. Unfortunately we are vulnerable and fragile, and people can do things they regret all their lives. Why some people decompensate in such dramatic and fatal ways, whereas the vast majority don't, is strange.

"It was a crime of passion. He was guilty but insane. He didn't realise his own strength". Too bad! The victims cannot claim mitigating circumstances. People become violent in this sense for many reasons. Maybe they ignore the warning signs. They have a house full of guns and they handle them and point them and the cascade toward use has already well advanced. Not everyone with a stash of guns will shoot people, but you can't shoot without a gun. Guns are high risk because they are lethal and available and can act within seconds in the heat of a moment with deadly consequences. When there was natural gas in UK hundreds took their own lives with it because it was also deadly and readily available. Guns like gas wouldn't kill if they weren't available. This item has more to do with a breaking point for violence and aggression. The experts (forensic psychiatrists) say that once a perpetrator crosses a certain line in the pathway toward action the forward push to accomplish the act is much stronger - the point of almost no return. However the main topic we are discussing is about survival and whether we all break at some stage from pressure and stress. The answer to this is no. Some people don't seem to break down. The following is a list of possible reasons why not:

- they have super genes that endow them with strength and resilience, the "warrior genes"
- they have been prepared by training or anticipation or by having to overcome obstacles in their lives
- they "came up the hard way" and are made of pure steel
- they get support and have many friends and are socially well connected
- they don't have vulnerability genes that predispose to illness or fragility of character
- they have a reason to live or survive and get through the ordeal, which could be a love, a career, a religious belief

- they have a meaning in their plight and see it somehow in a positive light (many religions see suffering as a way to connect with God)
- they have astounding motivation to overcome the obstacle and survive
- they have all of these or a combination of this protective factors

The world of positive psychology focuses on resilience factors and survival skills and virtues that are characteristic of winners and survivors. It tries to learn from those that don't become unwell when stressed. For example, 20% of the troops that returned from Afghanistan and Iraq to USA had post traumatic stress disorder. That means 80% didn't and positive psychology looks at the 80% to see why they "survived". Survival of the fittest according to Darwin is the basis of natural selection and only the strong survive and the rest disappear. This key stone in the evolutionary model of animal development seems logical. You could say the British have excelled in this respect and have a good gene pool because of their prowess at building up the British Empire.

The same could be said for Aztecs and Chinese and Romans who also had great empires. The dividing line between the contributions of good genes and of other factors, such as technical advancement, the possession of guns and steel and glass, and well trained and equipped armies, is impossible to tell. It could be said that if any race had the resources of Britain or Rome it also could have built an empire. Whether Britain or Rome possessed the resources because they were lucky, or more industrious, or more intelligent, or all of those factors, is impossible to tell. What you can say is that when they had the resources they certainly made use of them. Full marks for application!

Whether ordinary people living ordinary lives have warrior genes, or resources, or supports, or good preparation, or all of the above or none, determines to a large extent whether they succumb to stress or not. The other un-measurable factor is motivation. Some people do very well with significant disability whereas others with no disability fail in the same tasks. This comes down to the concept and reality of motivation. When a person really wants to do something, they pull out all the stops, and recruit all their powers to achieve and surpass themselves, and their capacities. It is very difficult to measure motivation but you can assess it retrospectively by the results it brings about. The psychology of the "drop out" and of the "winner" or super achiever is intriguing.

A drop out could be sick, he could have a poor background or family life, he may not agree with the enterprise e.g. army training, or he may be a wimp. An interesting angle from the spiritual or ascetic literature in the area of struggle and stress is the idea of humility and of childlikeness, and as a result the idea of asking for help, because the person realises it is all too much for them. This is a very widespread and utilised "method" for David and Goliath scenarios. Women over the centuries used similar techniques when confronting unequal opposition in particular from robust powerful men. Wisdom, intelligence, avoidance, running away, protection seeking and poison (!) were all used. Asylum seeking, refugee status and safe harbour seeking are all are used by people in distress and are appropriate. They are often life saving interventions.

The male suicide rate is six times the female rate in the western world. This seems odd. What is it about males that makes them more prone to taking their own lives? Suicide is the end result of many different pathways. Mental illness is a common predisposing factor to it. Alcohol abuse and substance abuse have contributed to large percentages of such deaths in every country. Stress and life events have taken their toll in this way during the recession. Physical illness can lead to it. In general happy people do not commit suicide. In general people with a good reason to live don't die by suicide. A full list of protective factors against suicide is available in suicide prevention websites and in standard psychiatric texts.

An enquiry into such male deaths, and these are mainly young to middle aged men, shows that they never sought help. They did not engage in ongoing counselling or mental health intervention. They never divulged that they were beginning not to cope. The vast majority of these men did not have a mental illness as described in psychiatric diagnostic manuals. They never visited a psychiatrist or even their family doctor with mental health issues. When they died it could be said that they had decompensated secondary to adverse life events, such as unemployment, financial problems, stress, alcohol abuse as a maladaptive coping method etc. Is this depression? Is it male as opposed to female depression? Whatever it is the end result is worse than with female depression since it is six times more fatal and therefore it requires diagnosis treatment and prevention.

Why don't men talk? Would talking cure or reduce the terrible toll of male suicide? What is the answer? A problem shared is a problem halved. Talking therapy does work. Managing one's financial debt, or one's marriage, or one's physical illness with the help of an expert all work. It makes the problem concrete and then breaks it into small manageable pieces. This prevents it from growing to enormous proportions in a depressed or severely stressed brain. When a person is stressed or depressed they often lose their capacity to judge and make decisions and they end up floundering in a sea of ever growing and overwhelming problems that seem to them to be insurmountable. This is the harbinger of "ways out of the dilemma" and this is unfortunately when suicide appears. This issue is being dealt with now because it is the worst breaking point a person can suffer. It is a widespread problem and affects an inordinate number of otherwise healthy young men.

The human mind and brain are vulnerable and easily injured and "unbalanced". This can be caused by physical trauma like a blow to the head or an accident, or due to mental trauma like stress abuse or neglect. Substance abuse and physical illness also impact on the brain/mind and can cause damage. A person with an intact "normal brain" navigates life ducking the bullets and hopefully trying to minimise brain damage from avoidable insults. However life itself has its own inbuilt wear and tear and to get to old age with ones brain and mind in good working order is no mean feat. Then the spectres of ischaemia and dementia lurk ready to make you forget all you ever knew!

The meaning of brain here is the physical organ. The meaning of mind is the abstract or spiritual dimension of the person which emanates from the brain and body but which has an independent existence, though still dependent on the brain for support to function going forward i.e. to do new things. The panorama of ailments arising in the brain is enormous. They can be structural like strokes and tumours and injuries causing loss of physical functions, and mental functions like memory and speech and perception. These physical abnormalities will not be discussed further. The chemical and non X-ray apparent and non physically caused dysfunctions of the brain/mind are less clearly understood and come under the specialty of psychiatry. There are some knowns. Multiple losses are said to cause depression. Fear is said to predispose to and cause anxiety and panic. Trauma either witnessed or to oneself causes post traumatic stress disorder and adjustment disorders. Childhood abuse causes attachment problems and relationship problems and self harming behaviours. Some types of childhood abuse causes disorders of personality. There is also the category of genetically caused or related mental illness. These occur in general without predisposing factors like stress, precipitating factors like job loss, and perpetuating factors like a difficult living environment. All of these factors are likely to make the genetic illness worse but do not cause it as such. Bipolar illness for example may have a life of its own and have highs and lows unrelated to any thing happening in a person's life. Schizophrenia also has strong genetic basis and will be present regardless of life events, but as with any mental illness adverse life events make all illness more likely to flare up.

The issue of resilience in mental illness is crucial. It is also crucial for people without mental illness. Some people talk about hardiness and protective factors. Not every child brought up in a care home is a disturbed adult. Not every soldier exposed to combat gets post traumatic stress. Not every bullied person becomes depressed. The list of established predisposing factors for mental illness is well known. They include: any head injury; childhood abuse and adversity; physical illness; genetic loading for mental illness; being bullied or stalked or harassed or abused or badly treated in general; any disease or infection affecting the brain; epilepsy; being a refugee or asylum seeker or homeless or destitute or malnourished; and the list is not exhaustive. Take all of these out of the mix and subject the brain/mind to 65 years or more of life and see what percentage succumb to mental illness!

The protective factors against mental illness include: genetic robustness; personality or personal strength; social cohesion and connectivity (having friends); family support; avoidance of known risks; suitable parenting; employment or occupation; adequate housing; opportunity to grow and develop as an adult. These are the characteristics in general of well balanced and socially connected people. We are familiar these recession days with the concepts of stress testing of banks and financial institutions, and that is what is happening all the time to our mental structures. The usual ups and downs of life are stress tests and are usually overcome with effort and experience and resilience and in the process we learn new skills. A really big stress or repeated stresses or a continual stress can cause mental illness in even the best brains, but not in all brains. In people with no family or personal past history of mental illness and good pre-stress health the chances of surviving stress are better.

Earthquake proofing of buildings, steel rods through concrete, hotel issue crockery all teach us something about resilience and durability insofar as we can achieve it. It has to do with flexibility and having capacity to withstand hits by being broadly based with friends and interests and having a versatile outlook on life. If you are too set in your ways or too rigid and can't take on board new things and new ways you can break more easily…in general. This does not mean you abandon key beliefs or principles or decisions. It has to do with secondary level attitudes and with being versatile and adaptable in our mindsets. It means a sense of humour and a laugh and taking ourselves a little with a grain of salt. A Japanese fable about trees illustrates this idea. The snows came and a big oak tree struggled and puffed against the enormous weight of the snow on its branches and eventually snapped and broke under the weight. A fir tree which was also covered in heavy snow on all its branches gave a small shudder in the breeze and all the snow fell off and its branches bounced back up to their normal position. The moral being that if you are versatile and flexible like the fir tree and not rigid like the oak and if you ask for help (from the wind) you too will bounce back.

People who survive being buried alive (the 33 miners in Chile who were eventually rescued), people who survived the concentration camps, people who survived car crashes, and major surgery, people who lose family members suddenly and tragically ....all suffer severe stress and have their mental reserves sorely tested.

What do they do and how do they survive? They do their best and they get family and friend's support. Like at a funeral when all the towns' people line up to sympathise with the relatives of the deceased, and this lightens the grief and spreads it out. It is then a shared grief and it is easier to carry and to be public about it and not to have to grieve in silence and alone. The coping with major stress and loss and grief is similar. It demands a plan for the long haul. It could be distraction like talking to people, like reading, like cleaning, like resting. It involves the gradual acceptance of what has or is happening and coming to terms with it and trying to make the best of it. There are often five stages of grief which Kubler-Ross described and these are denial, anger, bargaining, depression, and acceptance. This combination of reactions can be sequential or mixed all in parts at various times. It is a standard and human response to serious loss. What survivors of catastrophes like the Chilean mine collapse found is that discipline, a daily routine, contact with friends and people who understand, and taking one day or hour at a time forges a pathway to recovery. These miners all survived after three months burial a mile from the surface. They were lost to psychological follow up because they became celebrities and got plenty of money and they all went their own ways afterwards. They were physically and mentally intact on reaching the surface.

Medication and focussed psychotherapy have some role in the healing process following or during life threatening trauma. Medication and psychotherapy are very important for the long term management of mental illness be it life event induced or genetic. Men don't cry, men don't ventilate, men don't ask for help. These common conceptions of male response to trouble need to be changed because men have bad coping skills as suicide statistics unfortunately show. Men should cry, men should speak, men should ask for help.

People have their own ways of dealing with life's knocks. In general it is about sharing the pain and accepting help and assimilating what has happened and somehow incorporating the result into one's life. It involves the ability to eventually accept what is now the new circumstance of life and of starting to live again. Some people get depressed. Some people get dissociative disorder where they distance themselves somehow from reality. They may forget and not recall an awful event and so keep on living as if nothing had changed. They may block it out of their minds. This more commonly occurs with conscious or unconscious denial. With dissociation the person may develop a fictitious illness called a conversion disorder, they may become speechless or deaf or blind. This has the effect of focussing attention away from the trauma and onto a neutral more manageable and less traumatic area, and allows them to continue to live. Not everyone is a superman and not everyone can take hits on the chin, and getting sick may be a very appropriate way and safe way for some people to cope with overwhelming loss or stress. Being sick you don't have responsibility except the one to get well. You get help and attract caring and sympathy and support. You are listened to and your mental faculties are treated with kid gloves so as not to make the illness worse. People can and do die of fright and fear. People can and do get heart attacks and stroke from stress and mental trauma.

The mind or brain are the point of entry for such psychological insults and sometimes they need to be locked down to prevent an overwhelming insult getting access to the person with untold consequences. Illness can be adaptive and does not imply weakness or cowardice or copping out. It may be necessary for certain people to protect their overall wellbeing. That does not mean a person should seek to hide or escape stress by faking or getting sick. The illness we are discussing is spontaneous and occurs despite the person's best efforts not to get sick. The world of fictitious illness is different altogether and deals with people who feign illness for an obvious or subconscious motive.

Illness could be likened to a fuse that blows an electrical circuit when the system is overloaded, and thus breaks the circuit and prevents an electrical fire. Sometimes we blow a fuse when stressed out or when our system is overloaded and this may have the effect of preventing a psychological fire. This may protect us from becoming permanently damaged or even from dying due to overwhelming stress. This could be understood as the brain going into hibernation or shut down by developing depression, or anaesthesia like state (fugue) or unplugged by developing a dissociative state, or even by developing post traumatic stress disorder. The understanding of how post traumatic stress could protect the brain and could be an appropriate coping mechanism seems less clear. From a distance it looks more like the brain has taken a direct hit and is a state of imbalance as a result. People subject to systematic and long term trauma or torture and abuse and those returning from war zones may and unfortunately often do have permanent post traumatic stress.

To come out with our guns blazing from every challenge is a big ask for most people. We have to be prepared for all eventualities in life and be ready to do whatever it takes. In general we need to be a suitable fit to the challenge. At times a mantra repeated over and over can help our resolve like: "failure is not an option". We may have the warrior genes. We may need adequate training in whatever bootcamp is appropriate. We all need humility and self knowledge and to be good at asking for help. We may "fail" and get sick. Then we need to cooperate with the professionals to recover.

The bottom line is that everyone does not have a breaking point! In the book Man's Search for Meaning Viktor Frankl found that it was not the macho types that survived the concentration camps but those who had a reason to live and who really wanted to survive to carry on with the love of their lives. Many testimonies from people confined to solitary confinement and prisons show that inner strength can conquer the worst possible catastrophes. Traumatised and abused children sometimes develop resilient hardiness that forges strength and survival and they become strong adults. Wives and husbands of seriously sick spouses often mature and become strong people through their odyssey. These examples show that the brain and mind have extraordinary resilience. The millions of people with chronic illnesses show courage and resilience and self mastery of themselves when they live day after day with their disability. They never make the headlines.

Most people would become mentally unwell with such physical illnesses. The sayings that "you never cross a bridge until you meet it" and "don't count your chickens before they are hatched" mean that you shouldn't over or under estimate a challenge or your capacity to deal with it until it is upon you.

Often sick people say "If you told me this was going to happen I would have died and now I don't mind it, it is part of my life and I get on with it" Amazing!

The unseen and untapped human resources we may have may not ignite until the occasion arises. This is a combination of resignation to fate, to acceptance of it and of rolling with the challenge and even growing beyond it, and all of this takes time and patience especially with our selves. "I won't allow it to ruin or rule my life" type of attitude. Para-olympic contestants have this mindset. They play through the pain and focus on gold instead of bemoaning their lot.

A great protective factor and consoling factor when we are in difficulty is to know we are loved, that we are accompanied and cared for. Human sympathy and support are powerful healers and make the suffering more bearable. When we have this support from others and the conviction that we can overcome the suffering and we try to take the tiny steps towards recovery, we give ourselves the best chance of surviving anything.

One of the worst trials a person undergoes is when those who should care don't and ignore or sneer at the suffering they undergo. You can somehow accept and file away the hurt and damage done by an unjust person because you don't respect them and expect no less from them. But a son or a daughter or a friend that show callousness can be fatal and cutting. This is truly a difficult trial to be left to suffer alone and be rejected by ones very own. No matter what happens we all have a private space in our minds/soul where no one enters unless the person allows him. This is our inner self. There we can lick our wounds and think things out and even forgive and begin again and change. We are alone with ourselves and can find our peace there. Like a hedgehog that rolls into a thorny ball to protect itself, we too can go to ground and think our inner thoughts and liaise with our own personal source of strength and inspiration. We can divulge this hurt to our therapist our pastor and our God. These can comfort us and show us the baby steps back to recovery.

Some people don't break because they have warrior genes that fortify them against depression and from going under. They may also have been bred for adversity. They may have anticipated and trained and prepared for this day much like special army units train assiduously for a mission. These survivors of severe mental trauma are also elite army seals bred for endurance. Their spirit never deserted them and their resilience and strength has its source possibly in a team of supporters (family, friends, health professionals) or brothers in arms who are enduring the same ordeal; mutual support like climbers tethered together on a mountain. They may be natural born winners with warrior genes or more likely they have also a spiritual source of consolation and strength. They pray and ask for help.

No matter, people have to live. People will get knocks and people will suffer. The ground rules for survival are to know oneself, to know the challenge, and to look for help when needed. Not everyone is an army seal not everyone is bred for victory, not everyone has nerves of steel. But yes everyone can be a winner and everyone can survive and the keystone is to want to make it through. The long range view and the unbreakable commitment or determination to "go the distance" are also key supports against throwing in the towel. We can all win. We can all be victorious. We can all continue to live with designer supports suited to our needs.

There always is hope. Time does heal. Time does help accommodation to new life circumstances. Often the power is in our will to want to get well and take up our lives again. This motivation to succeed and overcome has a crucial part to play in recovery. When motivation wears thin and we are on the point of "giving up" that is when the alarm bells should ring and we should immediately seek help. Even to say to someone that we don't feel like getting help is a move in the right direction. When we don't have this will to want to recover we say so and strive with ice cream and jelly or whatever it takes guided by mental health professionals friends and family to move forward....and to eventually throw aside the supports and walk again even unaided.

It really doesn't matter whether we break or whether some people break easier than others. What really matters is that we get up. What really matters is that we ask for help when we need it. What determines our success in overcoming life's slings and arrows is our desire and conviction that *yes*, we can, we want to, and we will carry on and even conquer our demons and life, and forge a life worth living.

LET'S TALK ABOUT GOD

When all is said and done, it could end up as a faceoff between one group and another about the existence of God. It could be one word against another and there would seem to be no way to prove one opinion against another in the business of the ultimate meaning of life and the existence of God......... or *is* there a way? We could go on for ever shadow boxing about life and death and the meaning of it all, and trading philosophical and scientific and human argument, but quiet cool simple rationality like that of a child wins the day. It's the "emperor has no clothes" syndrome. A child says it (sometimes unfortunately!) as it is. "Hey Ma what's all that brown stuff on auntie's face? Why is that man so fat? Why is Mammy crying? etc" What is logical and what is meaningful and what all points in the same direction has much more honesty about it than the "well we don't know, it isn't proven" attitude. The "don't know" camp either don't want to acknowledge the reasonableness of the big data or else they are afraid to, or a bit of both. "There is a tide in the affairs of men, Which taken at the flood, Leads on to fortune. Omitted all the voyage of their life is bound in shallows and in miseries…" so says Shakespeare in Julius Caesar. Fortune favours the brave and there is none so blind as they that would not see. These are human wisdom and like all these proverbs they have history and are based on the real nature of man.

In order to plumb the depths of the ultimate questions we have to be honest. We work with reason and so we must be prepared to be reasonable! What way does our mind work? We didn't invent the mind or for that matter anything, that is, out of nothing. We have a very definite way of thinking and acting. Given these limitations we can only do what our capacity allows us to do. We could say that these big questions are way out of our area. We don't accept that way of thinking however because the whole history of man is full of such deliberation. We do think about the big questions and all generations to date have done so also, and so it seems to be inbuilt in our minds. Having said this lets get at it!

Begin at the end and ask what would answer all the questions. See if all the data agrees with this answer or is at least is not contrary to reason and that's a great start. To refuse to advance when all the data point in one direction is cowardice and it could also be connivance. The business of God and creation and the source and origin of the universe and of man is not a neutral topic. It is laden with agendas and bias and good and ill will and world views and denials. It is not forced on us to see the wood for the trees. You could be shown the shadow of a man and you could still deny that a man is there and explain it away......but the simple honest response is to acknowledge it is a man's shadow and therefore there is a man in the area. You could be shown a herd of seal and deduce that there are fish, even though you don't see them (because seal feed on fish and where there are seals there are fish), but you could deny there being fish because it isn't proven (and you would be wrong!). You could see a spider's web on the mirror of your car and deduce there is a spider around, or you could deny it because you can't prove it. When a whole series of such proximate hints appear and all point in one direction you could deny the existence of the truth they imply, or you could be honest and simple and say "yes that makes sense".

A child usually thinks that his father or mother made everything and controls everything. He doesn't think that things are not caused. He doesn't take things for granted like as if they were always there - just evolving. He wants reasons. Why this? Why that? Why the other? A child grows in the use of reason and in the truth of causality. He is constantly asking questions. Everything has a cause. If things didn't have a cause they wouldn't exist. You don't get a shoe without a cobbler, you don't get a smile without a face, you don't get wet without water.... everything has a cause. If not, the kids are all nuts! Then, instead of asking this, that, and the other, they would be telling us where everything is from and would be pondering the grandeur of the universe and feeling more and more at home in their evolving world. But no, they ask why, they ask where, they ask who? Thus they expand their knowledge and they do so by dint of causality and trust in their parent's knowledge. Thus the child's sequence is to ask causes and explanations from a trusted adult he believes to know the answers to his questions. An adult is a little more advanced but the same idea!

The "evolution" of the human mind is most probably begun in the immature human head i.e. a child's head. Why the mind and brain develops as it does is a very intriguing question. The pathway the brain and mind plods from tiny immature lobules of the baby brain in utero to the deeply crevassed sulci of the mature adult brain is like you see on nature programmes with time phase photography, where the flowers blossom in 20 seconds and the eggs hatch in 15 seconds and smolt turn into salmon in 25 seconds. The unashamed staring of the infant eyes and the endearing gurgle and smile capture the mother's heart. The child then begins to explore and try things and navigate and walk and talk .....and think. Eventually he learns to "think for himself". The mother or parent crafts the first wobbly steps in his thought process and like speech it tentatively gets stronger and confident and becomes independent. Every human on planet earth does the same (provided he is not unwell or forced into other thought control patterns…). Every human has the same progress of mind and thought. He expresses a "me" and a "you" and "mine", and at 7 or 8 years a right and a wrong, and a slap and a cookie. He expresses causality very early on with the innate question *why*. Why do children ask why? OK it's to learn. But why don't they know? What's the purpose of "learning"? What is the deal in slowly but surely learning the technique of knowledge and of how to gather it and be confident it is real and true? These become hard wired circuitry that last a lifetime and are the same for everyone. We have not seen a human being with a unique thought pattern which differs from the generic human variety, based on causes and rationality and proofs. The reason why, is because this is the essence of who man is. A rational being. Why it is like this "scientists" do not know because its not their area. It pertains to many domains like philosophy and anthropology and science and more. We are made that way. Who made it that way and why? This is the question underpinning the origin and purpose of man. This is where pure evolutionists, who say we developed from "whatever" over the course of billions of years to the advanced state we are in today, this is where they part company with the creationists who simply say God created us the way we are and the reason is so that we could seek Him out freely and love Him.

Meantime back to the child and the notion of right and wrong which kicks in at about the age of 7 years. The whole game then changes and an adult mindset develops. Life then becomes less simple. You can still ask but you may not trust the source, you may twist the answer, you may have your own opinion. You are not a tabla-rasa that accepts everything unquestioned from your parent. You now have experience and have been touched by life. You tell lies or untruths. You now have passions and influences and drives and weaknesses and defects. These all muddy the waters. Pure crystal clear reason and cognition is seriously hampered and blurred by all of these factors. A depressed or mentally unwell person is advised never to make a serious decision until well for quite a while. The reason is because their judgement is impaired by their mood or sick brain. A person is advised not to correct a child or another person in the heat of the moment, for fear of going over the top. A person is advised not to hang around with a certain bad crowd in case they become influenced by them into erroneous ways. We could find ourselves in a sea without a rudder or in the wilderness without a compass. Our minds become complicated and influenced and darkened by our weaknesses and those of others. The answer to this problem is to be simple and honest.

People are very sociable and are very influenced by others. This is normal. When the fashion is to do X then it becomes the thing to do. To wear Beat headphones going about town for example, and after a while everyone is at it. When you act outside accepted social mores you are scorned or ostracized and banished from "proper society." Imagine if all were practicing drug addicts in your housing estate and you weren't, well very soon you would get involved or else leave the area. Imagine all wore red shoes and you didn't, soon you would. This is herd instinct peer pressure and social cohesion all rolled into one. We are influenced by others. When the corporate attitude in a company or enterprise is to sleep around, drink and use "recreational drugs", you would be sorely tested and harangued to comply with the usual mores if you were to stay there. You would be forced to change your thoughts and instead of seeing this type of behaviour as "wrong" you would come around to accepting it as being alright and just a bit of fun. Your reason and mind set would be forced to change. You would now think differently. This is a problem. If in all simplicity your first thought about this behaviour was correct you have now denied it and changed it, not for better reasons or cognitions but due to peer pressure and behaviour. Reason therefore gets blurred by actions and influence. This is neither simple nor honest. To fight the corporate mentality or to leave the company are the two other options, and in this case you would have to suffer to keep to your conscience i.e. what you consider true and worthy. These are the honourable way.

When the stakes are higher, and are about the existence of God, the game could be life or death. The herd can drag the weak person to their side, but the convinced believer or atheist are a law unto themselves and will withstand the pressure to comply. They have thought it through and are adherents to their viewpoint. The believers against the non-believers. Isn't it surprising there are no the empirical proofs for the existence of God, and that may be because it is something to do with us, and also with God. If God's existence was provable and compelling in its proof, then freedom would go. There would be no choice but to accept God, and the phenomenal possibility of freely opting for God would not exist. This would undermine the basis of love, which is to freely choose the beloved. The reason God hides is so that we can freely search and find Him and love Him through the faculty and gift of belief. Why else is the world and man the way they are?

Let us diversify for a moment and work around the point. Kids talk about magic and Harry Potter and pantomimes. They imagine all kinds of impossible things and powers. They think these things really happen. They think Santa comes on Christmas Eve to every good child on earth, pulled in a sleigh by Rudolf and his team. Where do they get these ideas? Why do they get these ideas? Are they a throw-back to a vestigial memory bank of the way we used to be? Are these chimera from our distant past that eventually get extinguished by the cold blunt adult reason and adult sour grapes of life? Adults have lost the sense of wonder and imagination and make believe, because they are brow beaten by the experience of life and disappointment and failure. Anything that does not pass the test of our understanding of rationality is unacceptable and is treated as impossible and fictitious. This is not meant to trivialise our rationality because it is our way of working and thinking and has served humanity well. It does point to its limitation and our limited use of it.

This thought about children's imaginations is like going into a cave 500 years ago and sporting a smart phone and showing off all the apps and connectivity and functions. Much like the Indians are seen in films to wonder at the guns of the white man. We now know that smart phones and guns are not magic but advanced sequels of rational research. Why cannot the kids be right in their imaginary worlds? In another 500 years we may surpass even their wildest dreams. Once an idea is in our human heads, no matter how young and immature our heads are, these ideas are somehow reality based and at some stage are do-able or are capable of being brought to life, provided they are not irrational. We did not fashion our cerebral lobes or any of our lobes for that matter. We did not lay down our memory traces or sow innate ideas in our minds. We use the machine, which is the human mind, but we did not design and manufacture it. Who then puts thoughts in our heads? Who inspires us? Who puts "crazy" ideas in kid's heads? Who sews the seeds of future projects in our brains? Who coats our minds with seminal ideas and drives and passions. Who lights the wick in our conscience and shelters it? Who erects the lens of life over our intellect? Certainly not us!

Let's say I was walking down town and met a man who invited me for coffee. Let's say I opened my heart to him because I found him genuine and pleasant and interested. Let's say he began to answer my questions and explain everything to me. Let's say we had another cup of coffee and spoke more. At this stage I am enthralled. I am gob smacked and am glued to his face and every gesture. He has answered all my questions about life and death and the answers make sense. I ask his name and he says it is Tom. I question him about wife and family and job. He says he is single. I want for him to stay but he says he must be off. We meander down the street and there going into a church is a widow mourning her only son who was knocked down by a car. We go over. He looks at the widow and sees her grief. He puts his hand on the coffin and says "arise" and the young man sits up. He gives him to his mother.

Could this be our expert? But how? This is Tom from Bunkers Hill and sure everyone knows his mother and father and cousins. How could he have powers like this? Answer is: "all I know is that we were coming down the street and he met a funeral and he raised a young man from the dead. Before that he told me all I ever knew about myself and explained it all to me". "But he never went to school. He is from the working class and his father is a carpenter. I don't know! All I know is that he raised a man from the dead. Ask him yourself. Well how do *you* think he did it"? "He is a prophet". "Go way out of that, you can follow him if you want but I want proof and evidence". (This is a paraphrase from the raising of the only son of the widow of Nain in St Luke's Gospel by Jesus).

This must ring some bells somewhere! Yes it actually happened. Yes people didn't accept him and even his works, though they were out of this world. This really was the expert but people wouldn't and don't accept him as such. The amazing deeds he did were and are explained away and ignored. The result is that people still look for the meaning of life death and all the other unanswered questions they may have. They refuse to accept the incontrovertible evidence right in front of them.

The truth is that without accepting this man to be the expert witness, life will go on and on and it is back to one human opinion against another and this is not resolvable without proof. How do you prove you are right? You do it in three ways. You perform actions beyond human capability, repeatedly, like raising dead people to life, like walking on water, like changing water into high class wine, like curing illnesses etc. These acts display and prove superhuman power and knowledge. You behave in a way consistent with a perfect ethic and moral and law and love. You explain yourself, life and everything to all sorts of people so that they understand and are awed by the sublimity of your speech and knowledge and its penetrating truth. You show love and affection for everyone. Piece of cake! Any takers? The silence is deafening and rightly so. This is an impossible task which could only be done by….yes.. God.

Life's conundrums and the realness of God a creator cannot be proven and demonstrated by a human mind with forceful clarity and obliging acquiescence. What is possible for human minds is to show that the case for the existence of God is reasonable. It can be demonstrated by among other things the five ways of Thomas Aquinas, and from the witness of the lives of billions present and past who lived lives based on God, and from the reality of belief and its impact on the lives of billions. The absence of a real obstacle to this possibility is also important. The absence also of a credible alternative for the meaning of life and all it entails is also a powerful reason to tend toward God. The reasoning structure of the human mind with its basis in causality (nothing happens for no reason, everything has a cause, things always make sense) also points firmly toward God as the cause and creator of all, as discussed above.

Let us look at it another way. Let's say *you* made it all. What would you be thinking? You or I would probably be swanning around the universe with our sunglasses on, and the sun roof down, and no end of consorts to distract us. We would have won the lotto and party time for ever would be the name of the game. OR, being full of power and creativity and knowledge we would be studying our latest project, and tweaking it here and there with a few tornados or wars or symphonies or whatever. We would track each and every human and antelope and ant and living being and watch their progress. We would be particularly interested in man because after all he is made in our image and likeness. He is also free and you wouldn't know what he might do. You would scan humans very carefully to see if any of them actually got it! Does any one of those God forsaken creatures even engage brain and think: "Where am I? Who made me? Where is this? What am I? Who is behind it all?"

Does any one of those humans acknowledge me? I made the place and I made them and they never say "Hi". "What a crowd" you would think "I will send a tsunami and drown them all and just keep enough of all creatures to begin all over again and give them a second chance". Couldn't blame you! The problem is you actually got to like them and they are yours and you want them to guess you are there and are behind it all. You have spent 7 or so days creating them and are now tired and you really would like to get some thanks and even acknowledgement and wow! ......what about some love in return? You are sort of heart broken because the kids you reared sort of thing don't even acknowledge you. What you would really want most would be for them to love you in return for your loving them. So what are you going to do about it?

Yes you could send messengers to give them hints. Even better how about sending your only son. Wouldn't they recognise him and honour him? Especially if he showed boundless love and care for them they, then they would have to respond. Yes that's it, that will work! O MY GOD. Look what they did! They actually murdered him the only son and he so loving and forgiving and merciful. Sweet Jerusalem what will you do now? Lose the plot and annihilate them? "No I said I wouldn't do that again and I even put a sign in the sky so they know they are safe. I will have to talk to my son and see what he says". Bingo. And what do you know despite everything, despite being assaulted and ridiculed and taunted and humiliated and killed, the son said he would judge them himself, and meantime that it should continue until all the number of the intelligent ones (those who "get it" i.e. that You God are behind it all) are on board and are with us here. And so it was!

So far so good. What more could I have done? Nothing. It is just proof of the freedom of man. He really can choose to go it alone or to seek advice and take counsel. It really is winner takes all. You do your best. You want to give money for example to poor and they squander it and waste it and drink it and only a small number actually use it well and thank you. Freedom is similar. The chance to win serious spiritual money along with living forever along with perpetual happiness along with being at the top table along with actually being God! Absolutely beyond our wildest dreams. The sad thing is that so few "get it". So few actually engage brain and have the umph (courage or drive) to follow through to where it takes them. "I am sorry I made man" echoes from the firmament…and yet you really love them and want them to be where you are and see your glory. You invent a bunch of creatures and tell them "look no going into that area" and they do (Forbidden fruit). You can't have that. The machine disobeying the inventor. It is impossible. Punishment and teaching a lesson has to happen and checking to see if they mend their ways.

And so life goes on and those that will and want to, accept the evidence. "The words of the prophets are written on the subway walls and tenement halls and whispered in the sound of silence". Paul Simon says it as it is and it really is there "for those who *want* to see." What else is there? Life has all happened before and it will all happen again. There is nothing new on the face of the earth in that sense. People who try to explain life with human rationality alone are unidimensional. They are truly the flat earth crew. To discover what was beyond the horizon we had to go there, and lo and behold, we eventually ended up back where we started…and what does that mean? It means the earth is a sphere! How about that it never even crossed our minds, until we discovered it! What else never even crosses our minds? We didn't work out the earth was round we were shown it. We didn't rationalise that the earth was round, we discovered it. Likewise we didn't fortune tell that there was DNA at the basis of life forms… we discovered it. With more and more "discoveries" we then can engage brain and deduce further discoveries, like the discovery of penicillin leading to the world of antibiotics. Without the serendipitous discovery of everything we would never have advanced to the stage we are at today. One proof of this is that there are still tribes in the South Seas who were using stone tools until recently. Let's be honest, our progress and advancement are not the result of think tanks and human reasoning. Our reason works on what we are told or what we discover. These realities were and are always there, but we didn't know about them, and when we find them we act as if we caused them and knew about them all the time. Wrong. We would still be making mud huts if it wasn't for a gradual exposure of the wonders of nature to us. All we did was find it and then we began to think and work out further ideas based on these discoveries. Without new finds and insights and discoveries our minds would stagnate and even regress, due to underuse. We do and did not plan and map out the trajectory of the human mind over the centuries. It was pre planned by the sequential discovery of new things which then fed our minds and ingenuity.....but left to ourselves we never ever would have thought them or thought that way.

We are like children and it is as if our father leaves hints and clues around the place, and we find them and reach the present. Present, understood as gift, and also as the present stage of human advancement. Without the hints and clues we would not have advanced. How long did it take to invent the wheel? The Chinese advance in science stopped short because they never discovered glass. The western world advanced beyond all races because of steel which made tools and guns, and because of all the other wonderful *discoveries of the past 500 years.* Having said that you could well ask what man, whom some say is around for 7 million years, was at the rest of the time? The reality is that discoveries have fast forwarded man's technical advancement and have given him the answers to many of life's questions, be it in geography, physics, chemistry, maths or whatever branch of knowledge you care to mention. The clues and hints have been exposed to his intelligence, and in truth modern man has searched out their truth with causality and rationality and has found his reasoning to be true.

There are a finite number of truths about earth and the universe, and it is possible that at some time we will discover more and more. They are there, they don't change, they have always been there, and it is just up to us to *discover* them. Again this is reminiscent of the foetal brain lobes developing into child's brain lobes and then into adult brains. The history of man is similar. He has forged a system of thinking and investigating the world, based on trial and error and rationality, and has now a well developed adult human world brain. 5000 years ago the human world brain or the generic brain of humanity must have looked more like the child's simple brain lobules as far as knowledge of science and technology and physics and chemistry was concerned. The point being made is that the human method of thinking does work. It is true and does lead to advancement. It is also true that it is a search engine constantly advancing and learning new things by discovering new truths and then by building on this new basis.

A reasonable cause why the mind works like this is so that it also continually searches for the cause of everything, and it may take 5 million years like it has taken to discover computers and invisible ink, but it is plausible and not against reason....or is it? Well it is. The realm of causality points to a creation of everything, and also an answer as to how there was something rather than nothing. Why is there something? Why do we discover new things? These things were there all the time but we never knew. To ask why there is something rather than nothing is the wrong question. The question is: where did the things we see come from and what does that mean? The fact that something is there is already answered, we see it all around us. To ask why is there nothing, firstly makes you dizzy and then nauseous, and if you think longer the men in the white coats will be at the door, because it is an irrational question.

POSTSCRIPT

The ideas described in these pages have also been touched on and looked at from other view points in the two previous books in this series. They are The Human Mind and Belief – Opening Shots; and The Human Mind and Belief II – Unplugged 2013 and 2014 respectively.